THE HILARIOUS HISTORY OF HOCKEY

THE HILARIOUS HISTORY OF HOCKEY

Helaine Becker

illustrations by Bill Dickson

Scholastic Canada Ltd.
Toronto New York London Auckland Sydney
Mexico City New Delhi Hong Kong Buenos Aires

Scholastic Canada Ltd.
604 King Street West, Toronto, Ontario M5V 1E1, Canada

Scholastic Inc.
557 Broadway, New York, NY 10012, USA

Scholastic Australia Pty Limited
PO Box 579, Gosford, NSW 2250, Australia

Scholastic New Zealand Limited
Private Bag 94407, Botany, Manukau 2163, New Zealand

Scholastic Children's Books
Euston House, 24 Eversholt Street, London NW1 1DB, UK

Library and Archives Canada Cataloguing in Publication

Becker, Helaine, 1961-
The hilarious history of hockey / Helaine Becker ; illustrations by Bill Dickson.

ISBN 978-1-4431-0039-7

1. Hockey--History--Juvenile literature. 2. Hockey--Miscellanea--Juvenile
literature. I. Dickson, Bill II. Title.

GV847.25.B43 2010   j796.962   C2010-901692-0

6 5 4 3 2 1   Printed in Canada 116   10 11 12 13 14

Table of Contents

Game Opener 3

First Period: The Early Modern Era 25

Second Period: Hockey Enters
Its Pimply Teen Years 46

Third Period: The Modern Era Begins 98

Post-game Analysis 144

Index 145

Game Opener

AN ORIGIN LEGEND

Once, before the dawn of time and Wi-Fi, there was nothing but ice. Ice, ice, ice, as far as the eye could see.

Then along came a boy. He surveyed the vast expanse of white nothingness and said, "Boooor-iiing."

He said, "I will find a long hard stick that I can use to bash lumps of snow into smaller lumps of snow. I will then sweep my stick across the ice so that the smaller lumps of snow fly up into the air and spray my sister right in the kisser." And so he found a long, hard stick with a knobbly end — the First Hockey Stick. And he smashed and swept and sprayed the snow at his sibling until she was boiling mad.

She said, "I will find a small, hard chunk of ice and I will get my brother back big-time by kicking it hard across the ice at him. With a little luck, he will try to dodge the ice-chunk and slip and fall flat on his face." And so she found and kicked the chunk of ice — the First Hockey Puck.

But the boy did not slip and fall. Instead, he whacked the chunk of ice with his long, knobby stick. The chunk of ice rocketed right back at his sister. It slid right between her legs and into a hollow in the ice.

"He shoots, he scores!" shouted the boy. The First Goal.

The girl scowled and grabbed a long, knobbly stick of her own. She slapped at the ice chunk, sending the projectile right back at her brother.

The two First Siblings battled back and forth, back and forth, in an elemental struggle. They fought for control of the ice chunk, and they fought for the chance to score, and they fought over who had the better wrist shot, until day became night, and night became day.

At last, tired beyond all imagining, they staggered home, where they were scolded for not returning before the street lights came on. But the First Children smiled and were happy, even though they were both missing their two front teeth.

All was right with the world. Where once there was nothing but ice, now there was hockey.

HOCKEY'S GLOBAL ROOTS

What's that? Cave people didn't play hockey? You're probably right — but games of skill involving two teams hitting an object with curved sticks really do go back to prehistoric times.

Pyramid of Pucks?

Four thousand years ago, artists drew pictures of a sport similar to modern hockey in Egyptian tombs. The sticks were made with long palm tree branches that were bent at the end. The "puck" was made out of two pieces of leather stuffed with papyrus.

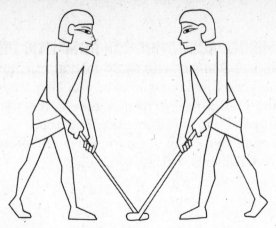

Greek Cheek

A stone carving dating from around 500 BC shows two teams of Greek boys playing a version of field hockey called *keretizein*. Those cheeky Greeks were playing it stark naked!

Ancient Roman Hairballs

In ancient Rome, people played the "ball-and-stick" game. Those with better vocabularies called it *paganica*. The game was played with bent wooden sticks and leather balls filled with feathers or hair. The facing teams tried to hit their opponent's target, such as a post or tree.

Since there was hardly ever any snow or ice in ancient Egypt, Greece or Rome, all of these games were more like field hockey than ice hockey.

GAME HIGHLIGHT...
Hitting stuff with a stick is a pretty universal way to
have fun. So no surprise that versions of early hockey
were also played in Asia (on horseback), in South America
(with deer bones) and in Iceland (with frozy toesies).

THE MIDDLE AGES THROUGH ROMANTIC PERIOD

The ancient Romans were really good at marching long distances and conquering other people. They brought the ball-and-stick game with them where ever they went, so it was introduced to lots of countries in Europe.

Some of those same countries, though, already had their own ball-and-stick games.

Hurley or (ahem) Hurling

Left-winger Jim McKenzie once said about hockey, "Half the game is mental. And half the game is *being* mental!" That's more than true about one of hockey's ancestors — the ancient Irish game called hurling. It was so bloody and violent back then, you'd have had to be crazy to play it!

The first written record of the game dates from 1272 BCE. A foreign army invaded County Mayo in Ireland, and demanded half the country from the local folk, called the Fir Bolg. To prevent a deadly war, the enemies agreed to have a hurling contest instead.

Twenty-seven players from each side faced off. Using heavy wooden clubs, they played "till their bones were broken and bruised and they fell outstretched on the turf and the match ended." The winners, those furry Bolg, turned out to be very poor sports. After their victory, they killed everybody from the other side!

More than two thousand years later, hurley was still a game for only the bravest or craziest. An Irish document from 1366 described it this way: "The plays which men call horlings, with great sticks and a ball upon the ground, from which great evils and maims have arisen."

Because so many of the players wound up badly hurt, the game was even outlawed for a time!

Shinty

Shinty is a rough-and-tumble ball-and-stick game that has been played in Scotland for almost two thousand years. It was considered a great way to train warriors for battle and encourage teamwork. According to legend, shinty was brought to Scotland by Saint Columba, who had fled Ireland — after getting into trouble at a hurley match!

You had to be pretty rugged to play Shinty. In 1892, a Scottish nobleman described the game like this:

> . . . *an equal number of men drawn up on opposite sides, having clubs in their hands, each party has a goal, and which party drives a wooden ball to their adversaries' goal, wins the game . . . This game is often played upon the ice, by one parish against another, when they come to blows if intoxicated, the players' legs being frequently broke, may give it the name of Shiney.*

In Scotland, shinty was a popular way to spend New Year's Day. Whole villages, with teams of up to several hundred of players each, would face off. They mostly used tree branches for shinty sticks. In places where there were no trees, they made sticks from bound stalks of seaweed.

Bandy

The game bandy, or banty, is a lot like shinty. It was played in England as early as seven hundred years ago. A 14th century prayer book also includes a picture of two children playing bandy. The name bandy comes from an old Welsh word meaning "curved stick."

Praying for a win? A stained glass window in Canterbury Cathedral shows a bandy player with a stick and ball.

Bandy was supposed to be played on ice. But English winters weren't always cold enough. Most of the time bandy was played on grass, like a very violent game of golf.

During a game, teams made up of hundreds of players would scramble through frozen marshes and meadows, whacking at the ball and at each other. There were no penalties called, so games often degenerated into bloody, tooth-spitting battles. Games could last for as long as 15 days, or until the swelling went down.

By the start of the 19th century, England was starting to become more civilized. Bandy, however, wasn't. Many of the players wound up wounded. There were umpires, but they would only make calls if a team asked them to.

Eventually, common sense — or somebody's really mad mother — prevailed. In 1891, the National Bandy Association was formed and official rules were set. Now, only 30 players on each team were allowed to beat each other senseless.

Bandy is still played in Great Britain, Switzerland, Sweden, Russia, Germany, Scandinavia and Mongolia. (Yes, Mongolia.) There's even a bandy association in Canada! Today it is played on ice, but with a ball instead of a puck. The rink is also much larger than a hockey rink.

THE DAWN OF HOCKEY

Back before that handy-bandy rule book was published, and way across the ocean, in a place called Canada, a game that was part hurley, part bandy, part shinty and 100% superior to them all was under development. It came to be known as hockey.

Native Games

Over time, the Europeans brought their favourite games — hurley, bandy and shinty — to Canada. Guess what?

Native peoples here already had their own wild and crazy ball-and-stick games.

The Iroquois people played a game they called *baggataway*. French settlers thought the baggataway sticks looked like the cross-topped croziers carried by bishops, so they dubbed that game "lacrosse."

The Mi'kmaq of Nova Scotia played a game similar to hurley called *oochamkunutk*. Oochamkunutk sticks were made from a very hard wood called hornbeam. Hornbeam is also sometimes called stinkwood, because it smells really bad when it is cut! (Maybe oochamkunutk meant stinky-hockey?)

The Mi'kmaq and other first peoples, including the western Teton Sioux, also played ball-and-stick games on skates! Mi'kmaq skates were made using long, sharpened animal bones that were shaped into blades and strapped to the feet using leather laces. The Teton Sioux skates were made out of sharp pieces of buffalo shoulder bone mounted on flat birchwood runners.

GAME HIGHLIGHT

Mi'kmaq woodcarvers earned a reputation for making the best hockey sticks. MicMac brand sticks were the most popular sticks used in the NHL from the 1940s through the 1970s.

The First Real Game of Hockey

So when did the darned game stop being a combo of all of these other sports and become our own beloved game of hockey?

Most people believe the game we think of as "real" ice hockey finally got off the bench in the early to mid-nineteenth century. There are lots of arguments, though, about where the first true game was played.

Contender #1: Windsor, Nova Scotia

Thomas Chandler Haliburton, who was born in Windsor in 1796, got the story going that hockey began there. In 1844, he wrote about his childhood memories of playing "hurley on the ice" there.

Was the game he remembered our own dear hockey, though? Alas, since Haliburton has been dead for two hundred years, we can't ask him.

Contender #2: Kingston, Ontario

Another guy, James Thomas Sutherland, said that Haliburton was mistaken and that what he'd played back in Windsor wasn't really hockey. Sutherland said that the first *real* hockey game actually took place in Kingston in 1855. Canadian soldiers who were stationed at the British garrison there played on the ice of a very frozen Kingston Harbour. There were 50 players on each team!

Naysayers say that the Kingston game doesn't count as the first *true* hockey contest. Why? Too many players on the ice. Instead, they say another Kingston game, played between students of Queen's University and the Royal Military College of Canada in 1886, was Real Hockey Game #1.

Contender #3: Montreal, Quebec

James Creighton was born in Halifax in 1850. He claimed that as a child, he played a game that he and his friends dubbed hockey.

Around 1873, Creighton moved to Montreal. He taught his pals in Montreal how to play his childhood game. On March 3, 1875, Creighton and a bunch of his buddies played the first game of organized hockey inside a rink. There were just nine players on each side, and the game followed written rules.

Creighton's game was played before a crowd of 40 spectators and was considered to be disgustingly violent.

Now that *does* sound like a real hockey game, doesn't it? But the voting is still open . . .

The Kingston Whig-Standard

A disgraceful sight took place at Montreal in the Victoria Rink over a game of hockey. Shins and heads were battered, benches smashed and the lady spectators fled.

Contender #4: Northwest Passage

Some folks insist that hockey was first played by members of John Franklin's crew on their expeditions to find the Northwest Passage. Their evidence? In 1825, Sir John Franklin, while on one of his Arctic expeditions, wrote: *The game of hockey played on the ice was the morning sport.*

Unfortunately, about 20 years later, Franklin's ship, the *Erebus*, got stuck in the ice somewhere near Cambridge Bay, Nunavut. Everybody on board died. We can only hope crewmen begging, "Please, captain? Just one more game of Arctic shinny?" didn't cause the delay that left them icebound!

Contender # 5: Richmond, Virginia, USA

Yeah, right.

And the Winner Is . . .

The Society for International Hockey Research (SIHR) has determined that the first documented game was played in — drum roll please — Montreal. They believe the rough game played by Creighton and his friends in 1875 was hockey game #1.

But wait!

Of course, as new information comes to light, the debate still rages. The SIHR continues to study new evidence from all over. Recently, there's been an important claim from Pennsylvania — in the USA!

When last heard from, the SIHR claimed it needed several more years of research, and free tickets to Leaf games, before it could settle the issue.

Wherever the game started, by 1890, it had spread across the country, all the way to Victoria, British Columbia. The ancient ball-and-stick game had, at last, become the true blue, through-and-through Canadian game.

Hockey had arrived at last.

How Hockey Got Its Name

Most people think that the name hockey comes from a French word, *hoquet*, which means "shepherd's crook."

Other people suggest that hockey got its name from an Iroquois word, *hoghee*, which was either the stick you used for playing games, or the injury you got when you were whacked by one.

Folks in Windsor, Nova Scotia, not only claim to have invented the game, but to have named it, too. A Colonel Hockey was once stationed at the garrison on Fort Edward. He kept his soldiers active and healthy playing games. The one they played the most became known as "Hockey's Game." Two guesses how you played it.

Could the term hockey have originated in Ireland? There's evidence that it did. In 1527, the "Galway Statutes" prohibited "the horlinge of the litill balle with hockie stickes or staves."

Whichever is the true origin, everybody agrees that hockey is a great game.

SATCHEL OF STENCH

You can't play hockey without hockey equipment. Here, then, we take an historic tour of Ye Olde Stinkye Hockey Bagge.

The Stick

The first hockey sticks were simply clubs with curved ends. They were made from one piece of wood and were short and heavy. In the early 1800s, a stick with a flat blade became popular.

Eventually, sticks became longer and lighter. They were also made using separate pieces for the blade and shaft. Today, sticks are made from different materials, including wood, fibreglass, aluminum or graphite. (That's the stuff in pencils!)

Going Bananas

During the 1960s, Chicago Blackhawk Stan Mikita partially broke his stick in practice. Claiming he was too tired to go replace it, he kept practicing. Surprise — his broken stick sent the puck whirring through the air like a heat-seeking missile! The puck also spun and curved in totally crazy ways.

Mikita and his teammate Bobby Hull started fooling around with all kinds of bent blades. They sat on them, warped them and soaked them in water, trying everything they could to get the best shape. Their new "banana blade," as it came to be called, turned out to be a not-so-secret weapon. It launched pucks at flaming-fast speeds of up to 160 km/h. Their twisted invention helped turn Hull and Mikita into top NHL scorers!

Fans loved the way the banana blades added speed and thrills to the game, but goalies were not so delighted. Toronto Maple Leafs Coach George "Punch" Imlach once said that for a goalie, trying to stop a wild puck was "like standing up at the plate while a base-ball pitcher without control throws dust-off pitches at your head."

Back when the banana blades were still brand new, Blackhawk goalie Dave Dryden told *Time* magazine that he believed goalies should be allowed to use curved sticks, too. That way, he said, "we can fire the puck back at them!"

Today, the size of a stick's "banana" is strictly regulated by league rules.

Hockey Tape

In the 1920s, hockey players began to tape their sticks. The tape helped improve their grip on the shaft and make the blade stronger. (The tape was also useful for fixing eyeglasses, sealing broken car windows and tying rivals to chairs.)

Shin Pads

The earliest shin pads were used around the 1880s. At first they were just some padding sewn into a pair of stockings!

Early hockey star Cyclone Taylor fashioned his own thigh pads from parts of his mother's – ahem – underwear!

Today's pads have come along way: they are made from polyurethane foam, and your mother wouldn't be caught dead in them — off the ice that is!

Gloves

In the olden days, hockey players wore either itchy woollen gloves or played without gloves at all. The first gloves made specifically for hockey came out around 1904. Called "gauntlets," after the armoured gloves knights wore, they became popular around 1915.

The Puck

All the old ball-and-stick games were played with — *duh* — a ball. How did hockey wind up being played with a puck?

The word puck comes from the Scottish *puc* or Irish *poc* — both mean "to poke, punch or deliver a blow." Hurlers, for example, would *puc* the ball with their hurley sticks.

Early hockey players liked to puc at stuff, too. They weren't too picky about what they puc'd, though. Whatever was handy would do: stones, wood scraps, old fruit, pieces of coal, even frozen lumps of cow or horse poo! (Maybe they should have called them "poo-ks . . .")

The first flat pucks were used during the 19th century. Their squashed shape kept the puck from bouncing off the ice.

Vulcanized rubber was invented in 1839. The first pucks made from the familiar black stuff were used in the 1880s. In 1886, the Amateur Hockey Association of Canada made the black rubber disc the "official" puck of the association.

"A puck is a hard rubber disc that hockey players strike when they can't hit one another."
— Sportscaster Jimmy Cannon

Ice Skates

The word skate comes from an Old English word, *sceanca*, which means "shinbone." No surprise, then, that the first ice skates were made from the leg bones of horses, oxen or deer. They were probably invented in Finland more than five thousand years ago. Used for hunting, they were smooth and slippery on the bottom and worked more like skis.

The first metal-bladed skates were made around 200 CE. A thin strip of copper was fitted onto the bottom of a leather shoe. The sharp blade cut into the ice and gave skaters much better control. At last ancient peoples could run away from grizzly bears while doing fancy crossovers and three-turns.

Around 1859, New Brunswicker James Whelpley developed a skate for long distance travel. It was called the Long Reach Skate, after a section of the St. John River called, amazingly, Long Reach. Whelpley's skates were the forerunners of the modern hockey skate.

Back then, boots and blades were sold separately. You had to put them together yourself using straps or keys. Now that was a major pain! A spring-clamp, introduced around 1880, made doing this a lot easier. Unless, of course, the spring got away from you!

Modern skates, which feature a sturdy boot and a permanent steel blade, were introduced in the early 20th century.

Helmets

No one really knows who the first smart hockey player was (i.e., the one who first wore a helmet). Hardly anyone did in the olden days.

In 1979, the NHL made a rule that all new players *had* to wear helmets. Before then, head injuries were as common as heartbeats. Even after Bill Masterton of the

Minnesota North Stars died of an on-ice head injury in 1968, what a player wore on his noggin was his own business.

Some players had real style. Quebecer Herb Scott, for example, wrapped a pink handkerchief around his head for an 1892 game against Ottawa. In 1905, a referee at a Stanley Cup match expected it to be such a rough game, he showed up in a construction worker's hard hat!

During the 1930s, the owners of the Toronto Maple Leafs tried making their players wear helmets. Most abandoned them after just a few games because they kept getting teased by fans, sportscasters and opposing players!

Some of the team kept wearing the helmets, though. One — let's call him "cue ball" — did it to hide his bald-as-a-baby's head!

Goaltender's Mask

According to sportswriter Jim Taylor, "Goaltenders are three sandwiches shy of a picnic. From the moment primitive man lurched erect, he survived on the principle that when something hard and potentially lethal comes toward you at great velocity, get . . . out of its path."

Nevertheless, goalies did not wear any protection on their faces until the 1929–1930 NHL season. That's when Clint Benedict, who was recovering from a broken nose, donned a freaky leather mask.

In 1959, Canadiens goaltender Jacques Plante got hit in the face by a puck. "Never again!" he said. Plante returned to the game in a mask he had already helped to design — a piece of fibreglass that was moulded to fit his face. The mask helped Plante go on a huge winning streak, and later launched a horror movie craze, in which the bad guy wore a Plante-style hockey mask!

"How would you like a job where, every time you make a mistake, a big red light goes on and 18,000 people boo?"

— Jacques Plante

Modern masks are completely made of fibreglass, or a combination of fibreglass and a metal cage. They protect the face and head of the goalie, but are lighter and don't impair the goalie's vision as much as the old style. Best of all, they can be decorated in totally awesome designs.

SO WHY DO HOCKEY BAGS SMELL SO BAD?

Every hockey player (and every hockey mom) is familiar with the stink of a well-used hockey bag. It can combine the fetid smell of a long-dead ferret with the fragrance of six-week-old cheese, cat pee, burped hot dogs and tuna-barf.

Blame the putrid perfume on a variety of vile microbes. For you, tossing your gear into the bag signals game over. But for bacteria and fungi, that's the start-whistle for a feeding frenzy!

Lots of itty-bitty critters feast on the mm-mm-good sweat players leave behind on jocks and jerseys. The more they feed, the more they reproduce, and the more microbes there are to give off their distinctive scents: gross, grosser and "who died?" The best way to beat the stink is to air out your gear immediately after you play — and keep it washed, too!

First Period:
The Early Modern Era

The year was 1887. At McGill University, in Montreal, the first official hockey club had just been founded. It was called, incredibly, the McGill University Hockey Club. Less than ten years later, the first amateur hockey league was formed in Kingston, Ontario. It wasn't long before hockey was on a Canadian breakaway.

ROAD TRIP!

By 1889, indoor leagues had sprung up across the country. The Dartmouth, Nova Scotia, Chebuctos claimed the honour of being the first team to set out on a hockey road trip. The Chebuctos went to Montreal to play two games against the Quebec Hockey Club. There was just one teensy problem: the two teams played by different rules! They agreed to play one game under the "Halifax Rules," and one under the "Montreal Rules."

Unfortunately, no matter which rules they played by, the Chebuctos couldn't score. They lost both games: 8–0 and 5–1.

The First Leagues Are Formed

With the game of hockey exploding in popularity, lots of people saw a chance to make some cold, hard cash. One way to do it was to hold games that people would pay to watch. Leagues began popping up like mushrooms in manure. The Amateur Hockey Association of Canada got its start in 1886. The Coloured Hockey League, which had only black players, started up in 1894 in Nova Scotia. The Ontario Hockey Association was organized in 1896 and the Eastern Canada Hockey Association dates to 1906.

MILKMAN'S SLAP

Indoor leagues were key to getting fans out. Before that, being a hockey fan was frosty work. For instance, spectators could be seen performing "The Milkman's Slap." To chase away the chills, fans would jump up and down in a frantic war dance, wildly flapping their arms and slapping at their legs, sides and shoulders. Anything to stay warm.

Although still unheated, indoor ice rinks made being a hockey supporter a lot more comfy. Goodbye milkman's slap, hello *slap*shot! Indoor rinks could also be lit by the newly invented electric lights, which made it easy to follow the game, especially at night.

Close-Up on Hockey Fights

As the turn of the last century came and went, hockey remained true to its rough-and-tumble roots. Fans flocked to see the fights as much as the game. The roughness of play inspired many jokes, including this chestnut: "I went to a fight and a hockey game broke out."

Why was hockey so darn rough? Maybe the absence of rules in the early days encouraged head-bashing. Or, maybe the chance to make money from fighting was just too appealing. Some hockey promoters even promised slugfests between rival teams' "enforcers."

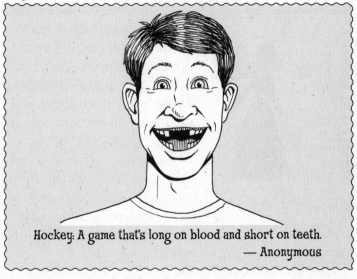

Hockey: A game that's long on blood and short on teeth.
— Anonymous

Just how bad was the fighting? Here are some early examples:

- In 1886, a game between Quebec City and the Montreal Crystals was so vicious that the Quebec City team had to forfeit. So many of their players had been injured, they couldn't finish the game!

- In 1907, after a game in Richmond, Quebec, the teams and fans got into a bloody brawl. A reporter from *La Presse* described the scene: "They beat on each other with hockey sticks, planks ripped from the boards around the rink, chunks of ice ... About 20 people were knocked down, unconscious and bathed in blood." Richmond's mayor banned hockey from being played in his city for the rest of the season.
- In 1910, a fight between the University of Toronto team and a New York team had to be broken up by the fans!

PROFILES IN HOCKEY

ISOBEL STANLEY

In 1889, Isobel Stanley, the 14-year-old daughter of Canada's Governor General, joined her father on a trip to the Montreal Winter Carnival. There, she and her family first saw hockey played indoors.

For Isobel, it was love at first sight. She and her brothers convinced dear old dad to flood the lawn at Rideau Hall (the Governor General's official residence) and turn it into a hockey rink.

Like her father and seven brothers, Isobel began to play hockey on the rink. Even her mother, Lady Stanley, sometimes joined in on the fun.

Hockey was a tough game for girls back then because they had to wear dopey clothing, like ankle-length wool skirts, turtleneck sweaters and fancy hats! On the other hand, these getups did give the gals one advantage — the full skirts helped goalies keep the puck out of the net!

Soon after the rink was built, Isobel founded the very first women's hockey team. Then, along with her brothers, this hockey pioneer convinced her father to help support the exciting new sport by donating . . .

Oh, Right! The Stanley Cup!

The Stanley Cup is the oldest professional sports trophy in North America. It was donated by the former Governor General of Canada, Lord Stanley of Preston (Isobel's darling daddy), in 1893 as an award for Canada's top-ranking amateur ice hockey club.

Lord Stanley shelled out $50 (or thereabouts, in old-fashioned British funny money called guineas) to buy a silver trophy. Its formal name was the Dominion Hockey Challenge Cup, but it was renamed the Stanley Hockey Championship Cup just a few months later. Today, the Stanley Cup is one of the most coveted prizes in the entire world of sports.

STANLEY CUP TRUE OR FALSE

1. The first Stanley Cup was made of gold.
2. The Stanley Cup was once drop-kicked across a canal.
3. The Cup was once kidnapped and held for ransom.
4. The Stanley Cup starred in a music video called, "He Shoots, He Scores!"
5. The Cup was inadvertently abandoned in a snowbank by the Montreal Canadiens.
6. Stanley went swimming five times.
7. A newborn baby was named for the Stanley Cup.
8. The Stanley Cup spent one night in a real igloo.
9. The Cup has been used as a horse's feedbag.
10. Goalie Martin Brodeur once ate chicken soup out of the Cup, calling it "Stanley Cup-a-Soup."

Answers:

1. False. The bowl Stanley donated was made of silver. It stood 18.5 cm high. The current Stanley Cup is made out of a silver and nickel alloy, it measures 89.54 cm tall and weighs 15.5 kg.
2. True — at least according to hockey legend. After Ottawa won the Cup in 1905, one of the team members tried to drop kick it across the canal! The kick was no good, and the Cup landed on the ice in the middle of the canal. The Cup was left there, at "centre ice," till the kicker went back to get it the next day!

3. True — again, according to hockey lore. It happened in 1907, but no one seemed interested in getting the Cup back. The disappointed thief wound up returning the Cup to the home of a photographer. There, the Cup was used as a flowerpot until the owner of the Montreal Wanderers finally came to claim it.

4. False. However, the Cup did appear on stage with rock legends Def Leppard — where it was shockingly placed *upside down* on a pedestal!

5. True. In 1924, after the Montreal Canadiens won the Cup, one of their cars got a flat. In order to get the spare tire out of the trunk, the Stanley Cup was taken out of the trunk and put down on the side of the road. When the flat was fixed, the team drove off, leaving the Cup in the snowbank!

6. False. It was only three times — twice in Mario Lemieux's pool!

7. True. Stanley C. Gordon Jeff Riley was born on May 6, 1997. The C in his name stands for Cup.

8. True, in Rankin Inlet, Nunavut, the hometown of NHLer Jordan Tootoo. The Cup has also ridden on a rollercoaster, visited Moscow, joined the climb to the top of *two* mountains and caught some rays on a fishing boat (where it wore a life jacket!).

9. True. In 1994 some of the New York Rangers took the Cup to the race track! They let the horse that had won the Kentucky Derby, *Go for Gin*, eat a snack of yummy oats out of it!

10. False. It was popcorn. The Cup wore salty, greasy butter stains until a teammate gave in and finally scrubbed it clean.

Early Days (and Nights) of the Stanley Cup

I Challenge You!

In hockey's early days, there wasn't just one major hockey league like there is today. There were dozens, plus more teams that didn't play in organized leagues.

This confusing situation didn't matter to Stan. The Stanley Cup was set up as a "challenge" cup. That meant that almost any recognized senior team could challenge the holder of the Cup. Teams only got to keep the Cup for as long as they kept winning their games.

GAME HIGHLIGHT
There were nearly 100 hockey teams in Montreal alone
the year Lord Stanley founded the Stanley Cup!

To prevent victorious teams from just kicking back and polishing their shiny treasure, a couple of independent trustees were appointed to keep an eye on things. They'd get together a few times a year to review all the challenges. If the trustees thought another team deserved a shot at the Cup, well, the match went ahead.

Disrespect!

Three cheers for the Montreal Hockey Club! They were the first winners of the Stanley Cup in 1893. But — get this, sports fans (or shall we say, get "dis?") — the winners from Montreal refused to accept the prize!

Huh? Here's the inside scoop:

The Montreal Hockey Club belonged to a larger sports body called the Montreal Amateur Athletic Association. The hockey club wanted more say about how the association was run, and saying no to the Cup was a way for them to protest their lack of clout.

The directors of the Montreal Amateur Athletic Association were *dis*mayed by their own team's behaviour. So the association decided to accept the Cup on the Montreal Hockey Club's behalf. And the directors decided to keep the entire kafuffle secret! (Now that's *dis*graceful!)

But wait, there's even more to this *dis*mal mess! The Montreal Hockey Club *never actually played a challenge game* to win that first Stanley Cup!

The Montreal Hockey Club had been the top finishers in their league, the Amateur Hockey Association of Canada. They were awarded the prize cup for that reason.

It wasn't long before lots of hockey challenges started coming in to the Cup's trustees. Over the next 17 years, there were 22 Stanley Cup challenges! One year, there were 4 Stanley Cup challenge series played!

LORD STANLEY, THE HOCKEY PLAYING ROBOT

In 2000, Lord Stanley won his first major hockey game. No, not *that* Lord Stanley, but a robot named after him!

The robot had been built by a team of college students for the Canada First Robotic Games. The robot could play — and win at — floor hockey.

The Lord Stanbot took home 10 awards in 14 different categories for his team. That was the most prizes ever won by a single team in the robot competition!

Great Moments in Hockey History – Klondike Katastrophe

One of the most celebrated Stanley Cup series in hockey history was played in 1905 when the Dawson City Nuggets challenged the Ottawa Hockey Club.

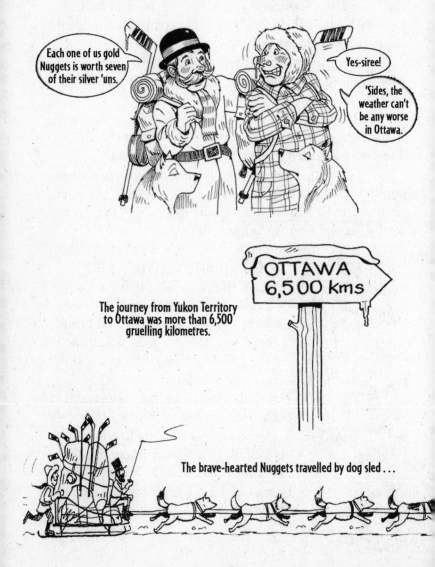

The journey from Yukon Territory to Ottawa was more than 6,500 gruelling kilometres.

The brave-hearted Nuggets travelled by dog sled . . .

ship . . .

and train.

A few members of the team went part of the way on bicycles.

This was a mistake.

For several hundred kilometres, the snow was too soft for their dogsleds! They had to walk.

The Nuggets arrived in Ottawa just in time for the first game of the two-game series. The exhausted team lost, the score a humiliating 9–2. The next game didn't go any better for the Nuggets. In fact, they suffered the most one-sided defeat in Stanley Cup History. The final tally was 23–2. "One-Eyed" Frank McGee, Ottawa's best player, scored a staggering 14 goals, a record that stands to this day.

Dawn of a New Century

The teams that competed for the Stanley Cup in its first days were amateurs. That doesn't mean they weren't any good. It just means that they played for love of the game — because they definitely weren't making money in it.

The lovey-dovey amateur period ended in 1904. That's when the world's first professional hockey league, the International Hockey League, was founded by — open wide — a dentist.

"Doc" John L. Gibson was from Berlin, Ontario (now called Kitchener), but as a young man, he had moved to

Michigan, in the United States. He was a terrific hockey player with an excellent bite and no cavities. In 1904, he got together with a Michigan businessman, James Dee, to found a new league that would officially pay players for their services.

To get the league off the ground, Doc Gibson needed great players. He headed to Canada to look for recruits. Signing up players for his league wasn't too hard. Canadian players didn't get paid in amateur leagues, so many were short of money. Besides, lots of players were miffed at Canadian team and rink owners who kept the earnings from ticket sales to themselves.

Once the International Hockey League was up and running, it was the Canadian owners' turn to get miffed. All the best Canadian hockey players had moved to the States! There was no one left to play on their teams.

Things got ugly. Some owners even threatened to blackball the Canadian hockey players who wouldn't play for their teams. (Maybe that's why the original name for a "faceoff" was "bully.")

By 1907, team owners had to accept the facts: whether they liked it or not, professional hockey, with paid players, was here to stay.

The Ontario Professional Hockey League, which skated out for the 1908 season, was the first fully pro league north of the border. Its nickname was the Trolley League, because the teams frequently travelled to each other's rinks by trolley!

The Eastern Canada Hockey Association, which had started as an amateur league, turned fully professional in November 1908. The rival National Hockey Association was formed in 1909.

PASSING THE CUP: STANLEY GOES PRO

The first professional team to win the Stanley Cup was the Montreal Wanderers. It had won the Cup four times already as an amateur team — its fifth time winning the Cup was the year it turned fully pro in 1910. But something about the professional league must have jinxed the Wanderers (perhaps they wandered and got lost?) — they never won another championship game.

During a 1910 home game against the Montreal Wanderers, Ottawa Senators goalie Percy LeSueur became annoyed by two back-to-back Wanderers' goals. He decided to do something about it. He headed into the stands to the fancy, expensive seats behind the Montreal net called "Millionaires' Row." There, he told fans it was their duty to distract the Montreal goalie enough to let Ottawa score! The fans went along with LeSueur's plan, chucking half-smoked cigars, programs and other junk at the Montreal goalie's head!

In fact, hockey experts say that a few teams paid some of their players to play as early as 1902. And, what a lot of people don't know is that *some* of the Wanderers' players started getting paid in 1906. This means that a lot of people, especially at the time, considered the Wanderers to be pros before 1910.

The End of the Challenge Cup

In 1913, the National Hockey Association (NHA) and the Pacific Coast Hockey Association (PCHA) reached an agreement. One of the things they decided was that at the end of the season, the winners in each league would face each other for the Stanley Cup. Lord Stanley's "challenge" cup would be no more.

Goodbye Stan, Hello Al

So what about all of those teams that didn't go pro? There were still lots of them, and they were left in the lurch — they were longer eligible to compete for the Stanley Cup.

Sir H. Montagu Allan stepped in. In 1909, he donated the Allan Cup to amateur hockey. It's still the top prize for senior men's amateur hockey in Canada.

Here Come the Canadiens

The National Hockey Association (NHA) got its start in a fight between rival team owners.

Ambrose O'Brien, the son of a wealthy silver mine owner, adored hockey. He had started up a team in his hometown of Renfrew, Ontario.

In 1909, O'Brien decided he wanted to play with the

big boys. He went to Montreal to ask the owners of the Eastern Canada Hockey Association (ECHA) to allow his team, the Renfrew Creamery Kings, to join their league.

The fat cat owners of the ECHA thought the O'Briens were pushy upstarts. They had no time for them or their little teams from the hockey "sticks." Plus, the ECHA was also preoccupied with another matter. The owners of the teams were fighting with one of their own, the owner of the Montreal Wanderers, Pat Doran. Doran wanted to move his team to a rink that he owned. That meant Doran would make more money from Wanderers' games. Other team owners, though, who split earnings from ticket sales with the home team, would wind up making less.

Playing it fast and loose, the ECHA team owners dissolved the league. They then reformed under a new name, the Canadian Hockey Association — without the Wanderers. And they wouldn't let the Wanderers in unless Doran followed their rules!

The Wanderers' team rep came storming out of the meeting. Who did he run into in the hotel lobby but Ambrose O'Brien from the Creamery Kings. Together, the two men cooked up a deal to their liking — they'd form their own league! They'd beat the snobs from Eastern Canada at their own game.

O'Brien and Doran then went one better. At that time, all of the major teams were owned by members of the English-speaking elite. Most of the players were English-speaking, too. A francophone team, the men reasoned, would be very popular in Montreal.

The league they created, the National Hockey Association (NHA), was made up of five teams. One of them was the brand new French-speaking team, the Montreal Canadiens.

GAME HIGHLIGHT

The Canadian Hockey Association lasted only a few months after refusing to admit the Wanderers and the Creamery Kings!

New Game in Town

The NHA introduced several key changes to the great game. They eliminated the position called "rover," where one player could roam wherever he liked on the ice. That left teams with only six players on the ice at the same time. Playing time was split into three 20-minute periods. The NHA also came up with the familiar system of penalties we use today.

HILARIOUS HOCKEY TERMS

Some of the lingo from the land of hockey is quirky and kooky. Can you match these wacky words to their meanings?

1. Bucket

a. Goalie who lets in a lot of shots

2. Bulging the twine

b. Goaltender, knees together, leg pads down on the ice — glove and blocker out.

3. Butterfly

c. Goal that hits the back of the net.

4. Chippy

d. The space between the goalie's legs

5. Dangler

e. Referee

6. Five hole

f. helmet

7. Sieve

g. Goalie's blocker

8. Waffle

h. A great stick handler and deker

9. Zebra

i. Aggressive, physical

Answers: 1f, 2c, 3b, 4i, 5h, 6d, 7a, 8g, 9e

42

WHAT'S A HAT TRICK?

Hat Trick: three goals scored by the same player in a single game. Originated as a reference to the jubilant behaviour of voyageurs who would toss their beaver hats when they successfully manoeuvred through tricky rapids.

OK, that's not true. "Hat trick" was first used in 1858 to refer to three goals scored in a cricket game.

In hockey, legend has it that the term dates to 1946, when Chicago Blackhawks player Alex Kaleta decided to buy a hat. He went into a Toronto shop owned by Sammy Taft and picked out a nice topper, but didn't have enough money to buy it. Taft made a deal with Kaleta. He said if Kaleta scored three goals that night against the Toronto Maple Leafs, Taft would *give* him the hat!

Kaleta agreed. That night, he scored not three, but four goals against the Maple Leafs!

In *1995*, Florida Panthers captain Scott Mellanby used his hockey stick to kill a rat in the locker room, then scored two goals in that night's game.

To celebrate Mellanby's feat, fans started throwing rubber rats onto the ice. During the *1996* playoffs, it was estimated that fans tossed $55,000 worth of plastic pests onto the rink! Now that's what you'd call a very cheesy rat trick!

Spotlight on the Habs

The Montreal Canadiens, one of the greatest franchises in hockey history, was born at the same time as the National Hockey Association. Here's some background on the beloved team:

- The Canadiens are the oldest continuously operating professional ice hockey team.
- They are also the only team in the NHL to have existed before the NHL was even founded.
- Since 1995, the Canadiens have been the only NHL team in Quebec.
- The Canadiens' first home rink burnt down in 1918. Its substitute rink also burned down — just one year later!
- The Canadiens' official name is Club de hockey Canadien.
- A version of the famous Habs logo was first used in the 1917–1918 season on the team jersey.
- The H on the jersey does not stand for Habitants. It stands for Hockey.

The Canadiens' first game was played before a sellout crowd against the Cobalt Silver Kings. They won in overtime, 7–6. The win was scratched from the history books just a few weeks later — when the newly formed NHA took in two new teams. They played their first game in the reorganized NHA just fourteen days later. This time, they weren't so lucky on the ice. They lost to the Renfrew Creamery Kings, 9–4.

The rest of the season didn't go much better. They lost 10 out of 12 games to finish last in the league.

GAME HIGHLIGHT
The Canadiens could be a rough bunch. A Montreal sportswriter was tormented by their pranks whenever he travelled with the team. They threw his clothes off a train and made him drink out of the toilet!

A Canadien by Any Other Name
According to legend, the first person to call the Canadiens the Habs was Tex Rickard, who owned Madison Square Garden in New York City (home of the Rangers). He came up with the nickname because he mistakenly believed the H on the jersey stood for "Habitants."

Other nicknames for the Canadiens include *Le Bleu-Blanc-et-Rouge* (the blue, white and red), *Le Tricolore* (the three colours), *Les Glorieux* (the glorious ones) and *Le Grand Club* (the great club).

A French nickname for the Canadiens' jersey is *La Sainte-Flanelle*. It means "the holy sweater."

Second Period: Hockey Enters Its Pimply Teen Years

The next decade brought even greater shakeups to the high sticks world of hockey. There were a gazillion leagues now scattered across the country. Not all of them could survive. As a result, between 1915 and 1925, most of the teams either merged or simply folded.

STAR LINEUP

Some of the greatest hockey players of all time played from 1910–1920. Or, if you prefer, some of the players with the greatest nicknames.

"Cyclone" Taylor was both fast and agile. He was famous for being able to skate and score backwards!

Didier "Cannonball" Pitre, "Newsy" Lalonde and Jack Laviolette were linemates on the Montreal Canadiens. Thanks to awesome speed and finesse, they were given the nickname The Flying Frenchmen. Cannonball's nickname came from his shot, said to be the hardest in the league. In fact, many of his goals were contested because they went right through the net! Newsy got his nickname from his early years working for a newspaper.

"Phantom" Joe Malone was the only player in the history of the NHL to score seven goals in a single game.

More great hockey nicknames through the ages — can you guess how they got them?

"The Chicoutimi Cucumber" Georges Vezina
Jim "Cement Head" Hargreaves
Milt "Count of Sauerkraut" Schmidt
"Old Bootnose" Sid Abel
Alf "the Embalmer" Pike
Hector "Toe" Blake
"The Missing" Link Gaetz
Gary "Suitcase" Smith
Bob "Battleship" Kelly
John "Pie Face" McKenzie
Dave "The Hammer" Schultz
Max "Dipsy-Doodle-Dandy" Bentley
"Teethpuller" Bill Carson
"Slumbering Romeo" Frank Finnigan

GAME HIGHLIGHT
New York Rangers goalie Steve Buzinski was so bad he
earned himself the nickname "The Puck Goes Inski."

GO WEST, YOUNG MAN

At first the Stanley Cup really wasn't national. All the teams that competed for it were located in Quebec or Eastern Ontario. But in 1910, that was about to change.

Frank Patrick and Lester "The Silver Fox" Patrick, brothers from a rich Montreal family, were both avid hockey players. Lester played for the Brandon Wheat Kings before winning the Stanley Cup with the Montreal Wanderers in 1906 and 1907. Both brothers played for the Renfrew Millionaires in the first season of the NHA.

In 1910, the two men decamped to British Columbia, where their family owned a successful lumber business. Out west, they saw an opportunity for setting up a professional hockey league.

The Pacific Coast Hockey Association got off the ground in 1911 with three teams. Lester controlled the Victoria team, while Frank was president of the league and owner of the Vancouver Millionaires — a name he poached from his former Renfrew team.

The PCHA was important because it made professional hockey truly national. It also introduced major improvements to the game: numbers on their players' jerseys and blue lines on the ice to open up forward passing.

WAR GAMES

In 1914, World War I broke out in Europe. Canada was part of the British Empire, and since Great Britain was at war, Canada was, too.

The war affected all parts of Canadian life, even hockey. The president of the Canadian Amateur Hockey Association, for example, urged every hockey player to join up. He said, "Canada will raise an army of brains and brawn from our hockey enthusiasts the likes of which the world

48

has never seen. The bell has rung. Let every man play the greatest game of his life."

Many hockey players took his advice. Some who went never came back. One of the many unlucky ones was hockey hero "One-Eyed" Frank McGee. Despite being blind in one eye, he had been allowed to enlist. To pass the eye test, he covered his bad eye with one hand. Then, when he was told to switch to the other eye, he merely switched *the hand* covering the bad eye!

Unfortunately, McGee's strength and agility were no match for German artillery. He was killed in the trenches at the Battle of the Somme in 1916.

Frank Fredrickson, who'd played hockey for the Winnipeg Falcons before enlisting, survived World War I by a hair. After his ship was torpedoed, he was found floating in the Mediterranean Sea on a life raft —according to some stories, he was wearing nothing but pyjamas and hanging on for dear life to his prized violin!

PROFILES IN HOCKEY

CONN SMYTHE

In 1915, nine players from the University of Toronto hockey team joined the army just days after winning the Varsity Championship. One of the new soldiers was a scrappy 20-year-old named Conn Smythe. While waiting to be shipped over to Europe, Smythe had time on his hands. What better way to spend it than by playing hockey? Smythe asked the OHA if he and his buddies could form a team to play in the Ontario League. To everyone's surprise, a huge crowd of patriotic fans turned up to watch their game!

In November 1917, Major Conn Smythe was reported missing in action. Everyone, including his family, thought he was dead. Smythe was anything but. His plane, nicknamed "The Incinerator," had been shot down by the enemy. He survived being shot at point blank range by a German soldier (thanks to a really thick coat!). He went on to spend 14 months in the harsh conditions of a German prison camp, where he was placed in solitary confinement.

Smythe survived the prisoner of war camp. He came home and eventually bought his own hockey team, the St. Pats, which he later renamed the Toronto Maple Leafs. He is also known for building Maple Leaf Gardens in Toronto.

Smythe realized that playing hockey and betting on it could make him a ton of money. After just a few games, Smythe had more than $5,000 in winnings in his pocket.

Soldiers Go Pro

With Conn Smythe and his teammates drawing strong crowds for the amateur OHA, the professional league, the NHA, realized there was plenty of opportunity for pro hockey-soldiers, too. In 1916, the National Hockey Association put together a new professional team called the 228th Battalion (Northern Fusiliers) Team. All the players were enlisted men waiting to be called up for service.

Five thousand fans came to watch their first game. Between December 1916 and January 1917, the Northern Fusiliers outscored their opponents by a whopping 40–20 over their first four games!

But then the inevitable happened. The soldiers were called up in the middle of February. They were off to war.

Just 10 days later, a scandal broke. It turned out that some of the players for the Northern Fusiliers had not really been enlisted men after all, but were "ringers." Star forwards Eddie Oatman and Gordon Meeking were not sent to Europe, and they admitted that they had been promised special favours to enlist! Before being sent to the front, they were given special discharges. And they weren't the only ones. It was a terrible disgrace for the army, the team and the NHA.

Keeping the Great Game Alive

As the war raged in Europe, the sport of hockey was in danger of dying back at home. With most of the regular players serving at the front, leagues were struggling to put on a good show and make ends meet. The Montreal Wanderers offered free tickets to families of servicemen, hoping to attract a larger audience. But it wasn't free seats that drew the fans. It was a new crop of top players from an unexpected source.

All-women's hockey teams had never been given the respect, or the money, of men's teams. Now, they finally got the chance to put their best skate forward.

Men and women turned out to watch the spectacle of women's hockey. Before long, the game even had its first female stars. Twenty-six-year-old Albertine Lapensée was one of the brightest. She played for the Cornwall Victorias, and was called by the Ottawa Citizen, "the queen of all lady hockeyists." Her own coach called her the "Miracle Maid." In one memorable game, she scored 15 goals!

Warned about Lapensée's punishingly hard shots, the Montreal goalie wore a baseball catcher's mask to protect her face!

Lapensée's hockey skills were so phenomenal that rivals began claiming she was actually a man. These rumours were only fuelled when a new recruit to the Montreal Westerns, 17-year-old Ada Lalond, did indeed turn out to be a boy!

Albertine Lapensée's hockey career was brilliant, but short. After scoring 80% of the Cornwall Victorias' goals in the 1916–1917 season, Lapensée up and disappeared!

SPOTLIGHT ON HOCKEY CARDS

The first hockey cards were introduced in 1910. They were included in cigarette packages, mostly as a way to help stiffen the box and keep the cigarettes from getting crushed! The cards had full-colour pictures of each player on the front, and some basic info about them on the back.

The cards were popular, but the start of World War I ended their career in 1913. It was ten long years before hockey cards were re-introduced. Their second life, however, was short, lasting only one season.

In 1933, hockey cards returned for a third time. This time, though, the cards were included in packs of gum instead of cigarettes. The gum company, O-Pee-Chee, was surprised to discover that the cards were actually more popular than their gum! O-Pee-Chee produced seven series of highly collectible cards from 1933 to 1941.

War interrupted once more, and hockey cards went back into retirement. In 1951, they returned, this time better than ever, with full-colour photographs of players and lots of action shots.

Today, hockey cards are coveted collectibles. They can sometimes be valued in the tens of thousands of dollars!

In August 2006, for example, a Wayne Gretzky rookie card sold for $80,000. In April 2007, a mint 1911–1912 Georges Vezina rookie hockey card shattered that record price when it was sold for $100,000! (A Newsy Lalonde card tied the Vezina rookie card price a few months later.)

BIRTH OF THE NHL

In the 1916–1917 season, the NHA was going through tough times. First, there was the ongoing problem of finding players, most of whom were overseas. Then there was the difficulty of attracting fans to watch the depleted teams, especially once the scandal erupted over the 228th Battalion team. And finally, there was Eddie Livingstone.

Livingstone was a double-dealing Toronto lawyer and owner of one of the NHA teams, the Toronto Shamrocks. In secret deals, he had arranged to raid players from the Quebec Bulldogs. Then he bought the Toronto Blueshirts without the NHA's permission.

Livingstone's behaviour enraged the other NHA owners. In 1916, it stripped Livingstone of the Shamrocks franchise. It then suspended his Blueshirts in 1917. Livingstone threatened to sue, which only made the league angrier.

Déjà Vu All Over Again

In November 1917, all of the NHA owners except Livingstone got together at the swank Windsor Hotel in Montreal. They cooked up a plan. They'd all resign from the NHA at the same time. Then they'd create a nearly identical league — but without Livingstone!

Strangely enough, a very similar backroom deal, put together at the very same hotel, had resulted in the formation of the NHA eight years earlier!

The new league was given the fresh and imaginative new name of the "National Hockey League" — or the NHL for short. Its original members were the Montreal Canadiens, the Montreal Wanderers and the Ottawa Senators. To get off the ground, though, they needed a team from Toronto. And it couldn't be Livingstone's Blueshirts!

Toronto Joins the NHL

The Toronto Arena Company owned a downtown rink. It agreed to hire the Blueshirts' players just for one season so the NHL could get up and running.

This team was supposed to be temporary, so no one even bothered to name it! Some people called it the Arenas. Others called it the Blueshirts or the Torontos.

In the end, everyone wound up calling it "The Champ." That's because the Team-with-no-name *made* a name for itself by winning the Stanley Cup in the NHL's first season!

STRANGE RULES

Until 1918, goalies had to stay on their feet to stop a puck. Falling to your knees was a minor penalty called "flopping." Goalies were charged $2 for every "Flop!" Goalie Clint Benedict got around the rule by pretending to trip and slip. Fans at away games would shout, "Get a mattress!"

OLYMPIC HOCKEY BREAKS THE ICE

When World War I ended in 1918, Frank Fredrickson, an Icelandic-Canadian from Winnipeg, returned from the battle ready to play hockey. But the top leagues wouldn't let Fredrickson or his fellow Icelandic-Canadians play! They were snubbed because of their ethnic background and kept out of the highest levels of Winnipeg society and sport.

Fredrickson and his buddies re-formed the Winnipeg Falcons, an amateur team made up of Icelanders. He had been captain of the team before the war and was able to get the old gang together again for the 1919–1920 amateur season. They also put together a new league so they'd have some teams to play against!

The Falcons won their league title. Then they beat the fancypants Winnipeg team that had rudely cold-shouldered them. *Then* they snagged the Western Canada championship! That made them eligible to compete for the Allan Cup. Their opposition? The blustery University of Toronto Blues. The Falcons blackened the Blues in two games, 8–3 and 3–2.

The Allan Cup victory was even sweeter than usual that year — ice hockey was finally being made an Olympic sport. The International Olympic Committee had decided that the winner of the Allan Cup would get to go for the gold!

HOCKEY ROARS INTO THE TWENTIES

With the troops back, Canada was ready to play. Professional leagues picked up where they had left off, attracting ever-greater numbers of fans.

Naturally, there were lots of games being played *behind* the scenes, too.

ON THE ICE AT THE 1920 OLYMPICS

- Ice hockey made its debut at the 1920 Olympics in Antwerp, Belgium.
- The ice at Antwerp's Palais de Glace was very small, but it was also very posh. Spectators could sit at dining tables at one end, and watch the game while they enjoyed wine with their suppers! A live orchestra even played throughout the game!
- The Falcons didn't have much competition for gold. Sweden didn't even have a hockey team until a few months before the Olympics — even then, most of its players came from bandy teams. They had to train with bandy sticks, wearing bandy skates and hardly any padding. Still, they were a tough team, and even though they lost 12–1 to Canada, they were the only team to score against them.
- The Swiss hockey team had more experience, but even they showed up for their 1920 Olympic match wearing snappy white shorts and very little padding. The goalie competed wearing a tie! The only serious competition came from the US team. Could that be because the 11-person American team included at least four Canadians?
- The Falcons won the gold medal after playing just three games. They returned to a heroes' welcome in Winnipeg, treated as stars by a town that had once snubbed them!
- After winning Olympic gold for Canada, Frederickson finally got to the big leagues. He went pro, playing for the Victoria Cougars. He led the team to a Stanley Cup win over the Montreal Canadiens in 1925.

Spotlight on the Leafs

Remember the temporary Toronto Arenas, who won the Stanley Cup back in 1917? Just two years later, in 1919, they were purchased by the Toronto St. Pats. In 1927, the St. Pats were in turn purchased by Conn Smythe, the returned WWI hero and hockey champion. Where did he get the money for the team? The same way he'd made big money before the war — he gambled, and it paid off.

He had big plans for his Toronto team. Inspired by a popular symbol of home among soldiers in the trenches, Smythe named his new NHL franchise the Maple Leafs. Next on his list? A new, larger arena. The fact that he had no money wasn't about to stop him either!

On the day Maple Leaf Gardens opened, a delighted Smythe wandered through the crowds of customers who were lining up to buy tickets. A nearby police officer thought Smythe was trying to jump the line. He grabbed hold of Smythe and escorted the team owner off of his own property!

In 1931, during the depths of the Great Depression, Smythe got Maple Leaf Gardens built in just five months! How did he do it? Among other things, he partially paid the construction workers with Maple Leaf Gardens stock instead of cash!

MAPLE LEAF SNAPSHOT

- Smythe wanted to call his team the Maple Leaves, but a minor league team already had the name. So he went with the less grammatically correct, but still patriotic, "Maple Leafs."
- The first Leafs jersey sported a Maple Leaf with 48 pointed leaf tips. In 1934, a few tips were dropped from the logo, bringing it down to 35 points. In 1967 even more points were dropped, until there were just 11.
- Owner Conn Smythe chose blue and white for the Leafs' colours because they were the colours of his old University of Toronto team.

Stanley Cupdate

In 1922, the Western Canada Hockey League (WCHL) joined the NHL and the PCHA in the battle for the Stanley Cup and things got really confusing. Two of the leagues' three winners competed in a playoff for a spot in the championship game, while the third team got a "bye" and went straight to the big game.

Luckily, the triple playoff didn't last long. In the fall of 1924, two of the three leagues, the PCHA and WCHL, merged to become the new, streamlined Western Hockey League. The WHL was now the only league that would face off against the NHL for the Cup.

The western league pit its league champions, the Victoria Cougars, against the NHL's Montreal Canadiens. The Cougars trounced the Canadiens three games to one, but the league's good fortune was not to last. Plagued by money troubles, it folded the following year after losing the Cup to another NHL team, the Montreal Maroons.

Now, in the 1926–1927 season, only one major league remained in Canada — the NHL. That's the fateful year that the Stanley Cup became the "property" of the National Hockey League (though, in actual fact, the NHL has to let other teams or leagues have a chance to try for the Cup in certain situations). To this day, the Stanley Cup remains the top prize for the best team in the NHL.

Here Come the Yanks

The year was 1924. There were four teams in the NHL: the Ottawa Senators, the Toronto St. Pats, the Montreal Canadiens and the Hamilton Tigers.

All of that was about to change. The Americans wanted in.

Trouble's Bruin . . .

Charles Adams was a grocery store owner from Boston. He fell in love with hockey and decided to bring the game to Beantown. The NHL gave him a franchise on November 1, 1924.

The first thing Adams did was to hire Art Ross as his right-hand man. Ross had been a star player in his youth, winning the Stanley Cup with both the Kenora Thistles and the Montreal Wanderers. He was also an innovator and inventor: he improved the design of hockey's goals and perfected the puck!

Adams asked Ross to name the team for a wild animal

that had speed, agility, and wiliness. Ross suggested the name Bruins, which is an old word for bear. Adams liked the name. It suited the team's colours, brown and yellow — the colour scheme for Adams' grocery stores!

Just one month later, on December 1, 1924, the Bruins played their first NHL game at Boston Arena. They beat the Montreal Maroons 2–1, but still wound up in last place at the end of the season.

AND THE AWARD FOR SHOWING THE MOST DEDICATION GOES TO . . .

In 1929, Boston Bruins defenceman Eddie Shore missed the train to Montreal. He hired a car and driver to take him the 560 km, even though a blizzard was raging. Shore grew impatient with the chauffeur's slow speed, so he took the wheel. He drove most of the way, only letting the chauffeur drive when he grew too sleepy. The chauffeur put the car into a ditch! Shore hired a team of horses to pull the car out of the ditch, then drove the rest of the way to Montreal. He arrived just in time to play the full game against the Maroons, even scoring the winning goal!

Stripes on Strike

Another new NHL team, the New York Americans, had its roots in Canada. You could even say the team "earned its stripes" there.

The Hamilton Tigers from Ontario won the NHL regular season championship in 1924–1925. You'd think they'd have been happy with the win, but they were anything but. The players felt the owners were taking advantage of them. Urged on by their outspoken centre, Billy Burch, the Tigers refused to play in the NHL playoffs unless each of them received a $200 bonus!

The owners and the league refused to cough up the dough. Instead, the NHL suspended the entire Tigers roster and awarded their rivals, the Canadiens, the league championship!

Headin' South

For the Tigers, that was "game over." Many swore they would never play again for their Hamilton owners.

Luckily for the players, new owners stepped in. A New York gangster named Bill Dwyer paid $75,000 for the Tigers. He also offered rich contracts to the players, way more than they had been earning back in Hamilton. Tiger loudmouth Billy Burch became the new team's captain and star.

Dwyer renamed the Tigers the New York Americans. He dressed them in dazzling red, white and blue outfits, which earned them the nickname "The Star-Spangled Skaters."

Talking about their first game in 1925, Montreal Maroons star Auriele Joliat said, "They looked like they'd come right out of a circus. We didn't know whether to play hockey against them or ask them to dance!"

Although they rarely had a winning season once in New York, the Tigers/Americans were still hugely popular with fans. But that turned out to be their kiss of death.

The team was so hot, it attracted the attention of Tex Rickard, the owner of Madison Square Garden. When he'd leased the arena to the Americans, he had promised that he wouldn't let another hockey team use it. But he broke his word when he saw how much money he could make on hockey. He quickly signed up for his own NHL franchise — the New York Rangers.

Sharing home ice with a rival team was really bad news for the Americans. So why didn't the team owner, Bill Dwyer, try to stop Rickard? Dwyer's hands were tied — or were they cuffed? He was serving time in a Georgia jail!

"Big Bill" Dwyer is certainly one of the more colourful

characters in hockey history. He was born in 1883 in one of the toughest neighbourhoods of New York, called, appropriately enough, "Hell's Kitchen." When selling alcoholic beverages was outlawed in the United States in 1919, Dwyer saw an opportunity. Using his connections on the docks, he embarked on a new career as a smuggler.

Dwyer outfitted his garages with secret doors, and his trucks with secret compartments. He paid off members of the New York Police Department and the Coast Guard so he could bring in shipments without interference. Within just one year, Dwyer ruled the bootleg booze business in New York City.

But apparently he didn't bribe enough people. In 1925, Dwyer was caught during an undercover sting and sentenced to two years in prison.

After his release (for good behaviour) he started to withdraw from the crime world. Dwyer built up his legal businesses, mostly in the world of sports. In addition to the Americans, Dwyer also owned a football team, a second NHL team (the Pittsburgh Pirates), casinos and racetracks.

Too bad he made a better crime boss than businessman — his legal businesses were never as successful as his crooked ones. Big Bill died penniless, at the age of 46.

The Americans vs. the Rangers

The New York Rangers shared Madison Square Garden with the rival New York Americans for 16 years. It was a challenge for both teams, but it hurt the Americans the most. Since their crime-boss owner had money troubles, he couldn't support his team financially.

Dwyer's Americans limped along for nine more years,

always on the brink of bankruptcy and in the cellar of the NHL. The team finally folded in 1942.

The Rangers, on the other hand, went from strength to strength. Their first team roster had been scouted by hockey guru Conn Smythe and included future greats such as Frank Boucher and Bill Cook. Another hockey legend, Lester Patrick, signed on as the Rangers' coach, bringing his expertise and enthusiasm to the young team.

The Rangers finished their first season with the best record in their division, and they boasted the league's top scorer (Cook). The next year, the Rangers won their first Stanley Cup, just two years after they were born!

In the 1928 Stanley Cup finals, the Rangers' goalie was injured and couldn't play. The team had no back-up goalie. So their 44-year-old coach, Lester Patrick, got between the goalposts, allowing only one goal in the next two periods! (That's out of 19 shots – several of them coming during sudden death overtime.) The Rangers won the game!

Hockey's for the Birds?
Red Wings and Blackhawks Join the League

Two additional American teams joined the NHL in 1926.

The Detroit Red Wings got its start when a group from Detroit bought the players of the defunct Victoria Cougars. The team became the Detroit Cougars but played its first season in Windsor, Ontario, because the home rink in Detroit was under construction.

In 1932, when the team was purchased by a new owner, James E. Norris, it was renamed the Red Wings. In his youth, the new boss had played in a Montreal league whose teams were nicknamed the Winged Wheelers. He adapted both the league's nickname and its wingy logo for his Detroit team.

THE LEGEND OF THE OCTOPUS

The Detroit Red Wings started one of hockey's most famous and funniest traditions during the 1952 NHL playoffs. At that time, you needed to win eight games to clinch the Stanley Cup. Red Wing fan and fishmonger Pete Cusimano thought that the eight legs of an octopus were a perfect symbol for those wins. So, to show his support for his favourite team, at the start of a playoff game he threw a slimy, squirmy octopus smack onto centre ice!

The Red Wings won the Cup that year. Was it thanks to Pete's airborne octopus? No one wanted to risk it. So every time the Red Wings are in the playoffs, octopi are thrown on to the ice at the Detroit arena!

The Chicago Blackhawks was the third American expansion team to join in 1926. Most of its players came from the Western Hockey League, which had folded the previous season.

The Blackhawks' owner, Major Frederic McLaughlin, had served in the military during WWI. His Infantry Division was named "Blackhawk Division" after a Native chief who held an important place in US history. McLaughlin decided to honour both the chief and his military past by naming his hockey team the Blackhawks.

GAME HIGHLIGHT

In the early days of hockey, refs couldn't blow whistles to start and stop play. Why? The metal whistles would have frozen to their lips in the cold arenas! Instead, they rang hand bells. Players and refs didn't like the ringing in their ears. A ref named Fred Waghorne finally did something about it — he introduced the plastic whistles that are still used today! A man of action, Waghorne was also the very first ref to drop the puck for a faceoff — before that, the puck was just placed on the ice.

Get in Line

A "line," in hockey, refers to a group of forwards who work together on the ice. Like "The Flying Frenchmen," the celebrated starting line for the original Canadiens, these lines have often been given catchy names.

Check out these other laugh lines:

1930s
Bread Line – Rangers' Mac Colville, Neil Colville and Alex Shibicky. The name refers both to the bread lines that formed during the Depression, when people were short of food, and the fact that the line delivered the team's "bread and butter" in terms of steady goals.

1940s–1950s

Production Line – Detroit Red Wings' Ted Lindsay, Sid Abel and Gordie Howe. Named for the way they produced goals, much like how their hometown produced cars on a production line.

Punch Line – Montreal's Toe Blake, Elmer Lach and Maurice Richard, because they sure packed a wallop.

1960s–1970s

GAG Line – NY Rangers Vic Hadfield, Jean Ratelle and Rod Gilbert, so named because they promised to score "a goal a game" (GAG).

1970s–1980s

Triple Crown – LA Kings' Charlie Simmer, Marcel Dionne and Dave Taylor. Why? Because these players were three Kings, of course.

The Hound Line – Toronto Maple Leafs' Wendel Clark, Russ Courtnall and Gary Leeman, because all three had once played for the Notre Dame Hounds.

The Brat Line – Toronto Maple Leafs' Tiger Williams, Jack Valiquette and Pat Boutette, because they were all quite young, and considered somewhat bratty by their teammates!

1990s–2000s

Crazy Eights – Philadelphia Flyers Eric Lindros, Mark Recchi and Brent Fedyk because their jersey numbers were 88, 8 and 18!

The Legion of Doom – Philly's John LeClair, Eric Lindros and Mikael Renberg.

The Mattress Line – Vancouver Canucks' twins Daniel Sedin and Henrik Sedin with Jason King. They were named for common mattress sizes: two twins and a king.

THE DIRTY THIRTIES

Hockey Night in Canada Gets off the Ground

The 1920s and 1930s were years of huge change. Among other things, they saw the birth of radio.

The first time a hockey game was broadcast on radio was in 1923. People who couldn't go to a live game could now follow it at home. That helped hockey explode in popularity. Listening to games together also helped knit the Canadian people into a unified country. Hockey — and Canada — was growing up.

Foster Hewitt, one of the first radio play-by-play announcers, became the most famous voice in Canada. He called his first games from a glass booth that was so tiny he had to keep wiping it with his sleeve in order to see the play! It was in this cramped booth that he first uttered the most famous phrase in Canada: "He shoots! He scores!"

After Maple Leaf Gardens was built, Hewitt moved to roomier quarters — a gondola that was suspended over the ice. The only way to get to it? A catwalk without hand-rails. On his first trip across it, Hewitt made the mistake of looking down — a full five stories! He went the rest of the way on his hands and knees!

By 1934, it was estimated that more than 2.5 million listeners were tuning into hockey broadcasts every week. The Saturday night show was so popular, in fact, that Leafs' owner Conn Smythe was afraid there wouldn't be enough fans willing to pay for seats in his arena! To keep them coming to the rink, Smythe made sure that broadcasts didn't start until 9 pm, after the second period was already underway.

The Canadian Broadcasting Corporation began operating in 1936. The weekly hockey broadcasts moved to the new national radio network. Now called *Hockey Night in Canada*, the show was heard across the country every week through World War II.

In 1952, *Hockey Night in Canada* also began broadcasting on CBC-TV. Television expanded the audience for hockey even more. It contributed hugely to the excitement and glamour of the so-called Golden Age of Hockey.

Today *Hockey Night in Canada* is a Canadian institution, watched in over 1.5 million Canadian households every week.

GAME HIGHLIGHT

During the 1930s, Elwyn "Doc" Romnes signed up with the Chicago Blackhawks. He had trouble being accepted by the team; sometimes they even refused to talk to him. What had Doc done to deserve this treatment? Nothing, other than be born in the United States! He was the first American on the team. Although the team was based in the States, every single player on it was Canadian!

You Can't Play Hockey!

The 1930s also saw one of the greatest dynasties in Canadian hockey — the Ranscombes. You've never heard of them? The story goes that sisters Nellie and Hilda Ranscombe built their own team, the Preston Rivulettes, after a neighbourhood boy teased them, saying "Girls can't play hockey."

That did it — they'd show him! And they did! The Preston Rivulettes became a powerhouse in the sport. Between 1930 and 1940, they played approximately 350 games, winning all but 345 of them (2 losses and 3 ties)! They were Canadian champions 6 *times*!

PROFILES IN HOCKEY

HOWIE MORENZ

Howie Morenz was one of the Canadiens' greatest box-office attractions during the 1930s. His play featured reckless bursts of speed and hurtling, head-long rushes. Morenz hailed from Stratford, Ontario, and his original nickname was the "Stratford Streak." He was also called "Canadien Comet," "Hurtling Habitant" and the "Mitchell Meteor."

Morenz starred for the Canadiens for 11 seasons. He was traded to Chicago and then the New York Rangers before returning to the Canadiens for the 1936–1937 season.

Morenz broke his leg during a game in January 1937. Tragically, he died several weeks later in his hospital room, at the age of 34, from a burst blood vessel brought on by the accident. His friends said that he had really died of a broken heart, knowing he'd never play hockey again.

During his career, Morenz scored 271 goals, won the Hart Trophy 3 times and was NHL scoring champion twice. He was elected to the Hockey Hall of Fame in 1945.

Tough Rivals

One of the Maple Leafs' biggest stars in the 1930s was King Clancy. He was called "135 pounds of muscle and conversation," because of his small size and outgoing nature. His frequent opponent was Eddie Shore of the Boston Bruins, one of the most universally despised players (outside of Boston!) because of his roughness.

Once Eddie Shore dropped his gloves and came right at Clancy, ready to rumble. Clancy dropped his gloves, too, but then stuck out his hand and gave Eddie's a shake, saying, "Why hello Eddie, how are you tonight?"

Clancy's quick thinking left Shore laughing uncontrollably on the ice, and Clancy's mug unscathed!

Think Shore doesn't sound so tough after all? During one game one of his ears was nearly torn off. He had it stitched up without anesthetic. He watched in a mirror the entire time to make sure he liked how it looked!

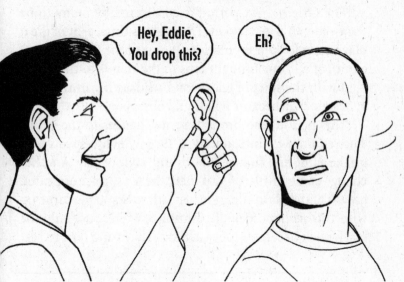

THE GOLDEN AGE BEGINS

By 1942, the National Hockey League was well-established as the premier hockey league in North America. Nevertheless, its fortunes had been badly affected by the one-two punch of the Great Depression and World War II. Unable to make ends meet, many teams folded.

The remaining teams were:

- Montreal Canadiens
- Toronto Maple Leafs
- Boston Bruins
- New York Rangers
- Detroit Red Wings
- Chicago Blackhawks

These teams collectively are called "the Original Six." They remained the only teams in the National Hockey league until 1967.

The Original Six period is considered by many to be the Golden Age of Hockey. During this time, a lot of great players made their reputations. Some of the most exciting games of all time brought fans in the stands to their feet. And with the start of television broadcasting in the early 1950s, hockey became a national obsession.

This period also brought some changes to the game. The red line was introduced in 1943, which helped speed up the game and changed the overall style of play. Another change came in 1949. Until then, the ice surface appeared grey, like the plain concrete beneath it. Someone came up with the brilliant idea of painting it white. Suddenly the black puck became a lot easier for players and fans to see!

GAME HIGHLIGHT

One of the fiercest hockey rivalries took place in the 1940s between the Detroit Red Wings and the Toronto Maple Leafs. According to Detroit's captain Sid Abel, "They pay us to play the other teams. We'd play the Leafs for nothing!"

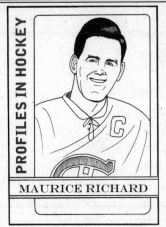

MAURICE RICHARD

If there was a player who could best take advantage of the newly introduced red line, it was Maurice Richard. His powerful shot and lightning-fast skating earned him the nickname The Rocket. In the 1944–1945 season, he blasted his way to a new record — 50 goals in 50 games! That record would stand for more than 36 years.

Richard was fuelled by an intensity rarely seen in competitive sports. According to goalie Jacques Plante, "First, there was the way Maurice would turn on his rockets from the blueline to the net. Then, there was his eyes, as bright as the glare from any rocket. Sportswriters described it as "The Rocket's Red Glare," a line pinched from the American national anthem!

Rocket Richard grew up poor in Montreal, and never saw a NHL game until he was actually in one! He spoke no English when he joined the league, and he represented the hopes and dreams of French-speaking Montrealers like no one else.

Richard also shared his fellow Québécois' resentment at a society that still discriminated against francophones. For example, the Maple Leafs' owner, Conn Smythe, once addressed a speech to "Ladies, Gentlemen and Frenchmen," and refused to let a French speaker play on his team! No wonder francophones were annoyed and French-speaking hockey players wanted to strike back.

Putting all of his passion and fury into his game, Richard stacked up some mightily impressive results. Here are some of his staggering stats:

- First to score 50 goals in 50 games
- First to score 500 career goals
- Led the league in goals 5 times
- League's all-time leading scorer (when he retired)
- Eight-time Stanley Cup winner, four straight as team captain

---

GAME HIGHLIGHT

When Richard was a teenager, he wanted to play as much hockey as he could. The best way to do so was to play on several different teams at once. But league rules forbade. So Richard adopted several fake names, including "Maurice Rochon."

Later, he didn't have to pretend any more. After a game between the Canadiens and the Leafs, broadcaster Foster Hewitt announced the three biggest stars of the game: "Maurice Richard, Maurice Richard, Maurice Richard!"

Richard was a great player, but he was also strong. He demonstrated his brawn in a 1943 game when Red Wing Earl Seibert literally jumped on his back, wrapping his arms and legs around the Rocket. According to the game ref, "The Rocket never broke stride. He went in, deked the goalkeeper, scored a goal and shook Seibert and threw him in the corner!"

A while later, Richard faced Bob Dill, an enforcer on the New York Rangers, who'd been given the task of stopping the Rocket. Things didn't work out quite the way the

Rangers planned, though. Richard wound up knocking Dill out — twice in one game!

> Another Ranger, Camille "the Eel" Henry was one of the smallest players of his era. During a particularly rough hockey game, he found himself brawling with one of the game's most feared enforcers, defenseman Fernie Flaman. As they fought, Henry shouted, "Watch out, Fernie, or I'll bleed all over you!"

THE FIGHTING FIFTIES

No matter how fierce the rivalry was between the Leafs and the Red Wings, it couldn't begin to touch the greatest hockey rivalry of all time — the one between the Habs and the Leafs. From 1944 to 1978, the two teams faced off in the playoffs 12 times, and competed head-to-head in the Stanley Cup Finals 5 times. The Canadiens have won 24 Stanley Cups, while the Leafs have won 13. Those totals put the two teams at first and second place in NHL history.

The on-ice rivalry was just one symptom of a greater rivalry between Canada's two largest cities, Toronto and Montreal, and its two largest cultures, English and French. Leading the charge for the Montreal Canadiens was headstrong, passionate Rocket Richard.

Tensions between the French-speaking and English-speaking hockey worlds came to a head in 1955. Richard got into a scrap during a game against the Boston Bruins and wound up hitting a referee. When he heard about it, NHL president Clarence Campbell suspended Richard for the remainder of the season!

In Quebec, Richard's penalty was widely thought to be ridiculously harsh. It put "St. Maurice" Richard's scoring title and the Canadiens' shot at the Stanley Cup in peril. Fans were so angry, a cartoon was printed in a Montreal newspaper that showed Campbell's severed head on a plate. The caption said, "This is how we'd like to see him!"

By noon the next day, an angry mob waving signs and chanting anti-Campbell slogans had gathered in front of the Montreal Forum, where a game against the Red Wings was scheduled to be played that night.

Canadiens' star goalie Jacques Plante liked to knit to ward off anxiety on road trips. He even knit his own underpants!

Even though Campbell had received death threats, he decided to make an appearance at the Habs game. The fans went crazy. They jeered and screamed at him. They threw tomatoes. One fan even punched him! Then someone set off a tear gas canister inside the Montreal Forum.

The Forum was evacuated. Fifteen thousand irate fans spilled out onto the street. All that pent up anger turned into a full scale riot!

Even more important, the "Richard Riot" triggered a new era in Quebec history. Many believe it was this moment that sparked the desire among many Québécois to separate from the rest of Canada!

PROFILES IN HOCKEY

GORDIE HOWE

Rocket Richard's great rival for the title of All-Time Best Hockey Player was Gordie Howe. In his final NHL season in 1980, he played in all 80 games and the All-Star game. He was 51 years old!

The man they called "Mr. Hockey" got his start thanks to an act of kindness. In the depths of the Great Depression, a woman arrived at the Howes' door looking for help feeding her children. Howe's mother gave her a few dollars. In return, the grateful woman handed her a ragbag of odds and ends.

The bag contained a pair of old skates. Gordie, who was just a kid, took them out to the local pond, sharing them with his sister. Each of them would wear just one skate! They would switch skates when their legs got tired. When his sister went home, Howe would get to wear both skates. That's when he would practice his skating and stickhandling skills.

At the age of 15, he attended his first hockey tryout camp. The Rangers' manager, Lester Patrick, liked what he saw, but before he could sign the teenager, Gordie Howe got homesick and left!

The following season, the Red Wings' coach snapped him up. He described the 16-year-old Howe as "the best prospect I've seen in 20 years."

At the start of his career, Howe regularly got into fights. He was benched, and his coach challenged him, "I know you can fight. Now, can you show me you can play hockey?"

He did just that. An all-rounder who could skate, shoot and stickhandle equally well, he soon was building a solid reputation on the ice.

All of his promise was nearly snuffed out in 1950, however, when during a game, Howe crashed headfirst into the boards. He got a massive head injury and almost died. He survived a risky operation, and wound up returning to the game stronger and fiercer than ever.

Howe was the only hockey player to play pro hockey in six different decades, starting with the 1940s. His final outing on the ice came in 1997, when he was 69 years old. He suited up for one game with a minor league team called the Detroit Vipers. He emerged onto the ice from the head of a giant inflatable green snake!

Howe skated just one 47-second shift. With that last shift, he set a record that will undoubtedly stand for many years to come.

Mooove over — The Zamboni Arrives

Who doesn't love the Zamboni?

The famous intermission resurfacer was invented by a Utah-born entrepreneur named Frank Zamboni. When Frank was a teenager, he moved to California and worked in an auto repair shop. Then he opened a shop installing giant refrigerator units in dairies to keep fresh milk cool.

Frank saw a cool new biz opportunity in the fast-growing sport of ice skating. Since there wasn't much ice in southern California (duh!), he decided to open an indoor-skating rink. He called it Iceland.

There was just one problem. Keeping the ice clean and smooth for skaters took a lot of work and a lot of time. Back then, the only way to do it was like this:

1. Get a tractor.
2. Drag huge scraper behind tractor to remove top layer of cruddy ice.
3. Convince three or four people to follow behind the scraper with shovels and scoop away the "snow."
4. Spray fresh water over the scraped surface.
5. Squeegee the whole darn thing, then wait for the water to refreeze.

That process took over an hour!

Every minute spent fixing the ice meant less time available for sale to paying customers. Frank's solution was to combine his auto-repair experience with his refrigerator smarts. He built the first Zamboni using a war surplus jeep and spare parts! *Ta-da!* A scraper/freezer on wheels! He sold his first machine in 1950.

Norwegian ice skater and Hollywood movie star Sonja Henie saw the Zamboni. It was love at first sight. She ordered one for a rink in Chicago, halfway across the country. Frank Zamboni drove it to her, in the dead of winter! He rode in the jeep he made it from, hauling the parts behind him in a trailer. It was so cold, Zamboni said, that he nearly froze!

The Zamboni made a big difference to the hockey world. Since rinks could be cleaned up faster and easier, pro hockey got more action and less thumb-twiddling. And all around North America, more kids could take up the sport and get more ice time. The Zamboni helped the sport of hockey gain popularity in the '50s and '60s.

Great Games in Hockey History — April 8, 1952

The April 8, 1952 Stanley Cup semi-final game between the Canadiens and the Boston Bruins has been described by hockey wonks as "the most beautiful in the history of the world." While it may not have been beautiful, it certainly was memorable!

With the series tied up at 3-3, Rocket Richard takes a knee to the head from Bruins defenseman Bill Quakenbush in the second period.

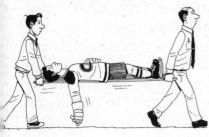

Richard is carried out, unconscious!

Richard returns to the bench in the third period with a concussion. He's dazed and confused, but he's still Rocket Richard.

Suddenly, Richard skates out in front of the net, startling Bruins goalie "Sugar Jim" Henry. Richard slips the puck behind Sugar Jim and into the net!

Richard doesn't even know what happened. After the game he says, "I heard the crowd yell and by that time I was too dizzy even to see!"

THE BIG SIXTIES

It's Getting Drafty in Here

In the early days of hockey, the way to snag the best players was to keep an eye on the junior leagues. NHL teams would "sponsor" a junior team — give them money — in exchange for the pro rights to any of their players.

This system started to change in 1963, when it was decided that hockey needed a fairer way to find and sign new players. The "draft" system was introduced. It worked like this: the weakest team from the previous season was given the first chance to select any of the available players. The strongest team got the last pick.

This meant that less successful — and less wealthy — teams got a shot at the best players. The draft system ensured team rosters would be more even, and therefore helped boost the level of league play.

GAME HIGHLIGHT

During a slump in the Maple Leafs' 1963–1964 season, a radio announcer jokingly suggested they needed someone to "put a hex on the opposition." That's when Mabel Leaf, the CHUM Witch, was born. The witch, played by a Toronto actress, cast her spell before the next Leafs game, and the Leafs won! They kept winning too, beginning an 11–2–1 streak with Mabel the Witch in attendance at their games.

The 1964 Leafs went on to take the Stanley Cup. In a post-game TV interview, star goalie Johnny Bower gave an extra-special thank you to Mabel Leaf, the CHUM Witch, for her contributions to their victory!

PROFILES IN HOCKEY

BOBBY HULL

On March 12, 1966, Bobby Hull made history when he scored his 51st goal and surpassed Maurice Richard and Bernie Geoffrion for the greatest number of goals scored in an entire season.

Hull's historic shot — timed at speeds of nearly 200 km/h — was not surprising to anyone who'd followed his career. Even as a kid, he had exceptional skills, combining speed (he was once clocked skating at almost 50 km/h) with strength.

Hull developed his skills by playing — a lot. He was always the first one out on the ice for a game of shinny, and the last one to leave. At the age of 10, he was a star on his Bantam hockey team. But after the game ended, he didn't go home like the rest of the kids. Instead, he'd skate out with the older Midget team that was playing in the next game! After that game, he'd go back out *again* with the even older Juvenile League players. Sometimes he'd play all morning, scoring up to 25 goals in 4 different leagues!

Bobby Hull was just 11 when he was scouted by the Chicago Blackhawks. They decided to lock him in to their program there and then. They convinced his father to sign a "C-Form," which made the young player the "property" of the Blackhawks if he ever decided to go pro.

At 14, the Blackhawks sent Hull to their Hespeler, Ontario, junior farm club, where he honed his skills. He spent the next few years bouncing from one junior team to the next under the eye of the Hawk scouts.

Those years were hard on him. He lived with strange families and in boarding houses, studied in four different high schools and graduated from none. He was a rambunctious teenager and missed the security and steadiness of home and family.

One evening, in 1957, when Bobby was just 18, he got a phone call from the Blackhawks. They wanted him to suit up! The Hawks were playing an exhibition game nearby against the New York Rangers that night, and they wanted Bobby on the ice!

Bobby knew this was his chance to get to the big leagues. So he choked down his supper and raced to the rink. He wound up scoring not one but *two* goals against the Rangers. He was moved up to the major leagues that very night!

The "Golden Jet" was a much needed ray of hope for the struggling Blackhawks. They had missed the play-offs in 10 of the 11 previous seasons and were desperate for a break. Hull was just the ticket. Alongside team-mate Stan Mikita, he began to change the Blackhawks' fortunes.

By the end of the 1959–60 season, Hull had his first scoring title, having earned 39 goals and 42 assists. In 1961, he scored 14 points in the post-season and led the Hawks to their first Stanley Cup win since 1938!

During his time in the NHL, Bobby Hull won the Art Ross trophy 3 times, led the league in goal scoring seven times, was voted league MVP twice and was selected for the All-Star team 12 times. By his final NHL season, he had scored 50 goals or more in a season an eye-popping 5 times!

But Bobby Hull was more than just a stat collector. His style of play, which was both brash and polished at the same time, embodied a new kind of hockey — one that was more exciting than ever to watch. Hull's greatest achievement was that he made a hockey fan out of every-one who saw him play.

The "Forever Rivals" Face off

Two teams dominated the sport of hockey during the 1960s: the Toronto Maple Leafs and the Montreal Cana-diens. The Canadiens won the Cup five times and the Leafs won it four. Both teams were in the semi-finals or quarter-finals nine out of ten times. This made for one hot rivalry!

The "Cold War on Ice" between the Canadiens and the Leafs reached its peak in the 1967 battle for the

Stanley Cup. It was one of the most intense playoff series of all time.

The two fierce rivals had only rarely faced each other in the finals, although they had met many, many times during regular season and semi-final play. But in the spring of 1967, the two staunch enemies were finally going to go nose to nose for the ultimate prize.

The Habs had a young and feisty team who had won the last two Stanley Cups. The Leafs, on the other hand, were relying on veterans who many thought were past their prime. The Leafs were even labelled "The Over-the-Hill Gang." The Habs, therefore, were heavily favoured to win. The Canadiens were so sure of victory, in fact, that the mayor of Montreal even built a trophy case to show off the cup at Expo 67 in Montreal!

Would victory go to the confident Canadiens, or the battle-hardened Leafs?

HORTON HEARS A WHO (HAS THE DONUTS?)

One of the most popular players on the '67 Leafs was the big defenceman, Tim Horton. He was huge and strong, but gentle. His trademark move was the Horton Hug, in which he wrapped his arms around opponents to stop them rather than crushing them with a hard hit.

In 1955, Tim's leg was badly broken. Unable to play hockey until he recovered, he went to work in the office of Conn Smythe's gravel company. That's when he realized that another injury could end his career in a split second. He'd better find another way to make a living just in case! One way to do it was with a doughnut shop. The chain of restaurants he founded — Tim Horton's — now extends from coast to coast!

Great Games in Hockey History —

Game 1 of the Stanley Cup Finals. The Habs trounce the Leafs 6–2.

"That's the Leafs' average age: 31 x 2 = 62!"

The Leafs aren't out yet, though. In game 2, goalie Terry Sawchuk shuts out the Habs 3–0.

"That's the Habs' average IQ – 30!"

In game 3, Bob Pulford scores the winning goal in overtime for the Leafs. They now lead the series 2–1.

The Habs tie the series back up in game 4 by winning decisively, 6–2

The 1967 Stanley Cup Final

In game 5, the Leafs dominate and win the game 4-1.

Game 6 is a real nail-biter. With just 55 seconds to play in the third period, the Leafs are up 2-1. All they have to do is keep the Habs from scoring.

The two teams face off in the Leaf end. The Leafs' coach sends in 42-year-old defenceman Allan Stanley to do the job.

The ref drops the puck, and Stanley wins the faceoff! The puck finds its way to George Armstrong. Armstrong puts the puck in the Habs' empty net to seal the win!

Toronto Maple Leafs: 1966-1967 Stanley Cup Champions!

Hey! Where Did All the Girls Go?

Remember back in the Dirty Thirties, when the Preston Rivulettes made history with their incredible hockey streak? By the 1950s, their feat was all but forgotten. Now Canadians returning from the battlefields of Europe wanted all the comforts of home — and someone in that home to take care of them. So women, who'd played while World War II was on, were kicked off the ice and told hockey wasn't something "nice girls" did.

Plenty of girls knew better. But it was hard to prove your skills if nobody let you on the ice!

Abby Hoffman began skating at the age of three and playing hockey with her brothers at five. When she was eight, she was keen to play on a team, just like her older brothers, but there were no girls' teams in Toronto. So she did the only logical thing: she signed up for a local boys' team — as a boy!

No one noticed that Abby wasn't "one of the guys." Because she was an avid swimmer, she had short hair. She came to the rink already dressed in hockey gear, just like all of her teammates. On the ice, she played just as well as the boys, if not better!

Abby's team won their league championship in 1955, thanks in no small part to Abby's strong skills on defence. She even wound up being selected for the Little Toronto Hockey League's all-star team!

That's when the snow hit the Zamboni fan. A closer check of Abby's birth certificate revealed her full name was "Abigail."

A scandal broke out and Abby became a star overnight. She was interviewed in all the newspapers and on radio and TV. All the attention didn't help, though. Abby sued the league for the right to play hockey. In 1956, the case went all the way to the Ontario Supreme Court. The court ruled against her! Since there were still no girls' teams, Abby had to give up playing competitive hockey for good.

Abby still loved sports, though, so she took up running. She competed in four Olympic Games in track and field. She even carried the flag for Canada at the 1976 games.

Despite her success on the track, Abby never forgot how she was robbed of her chance to play hockey. When she grew up, she chose a career in which she could help other young women get the chances she was denied. She worked for both the Ontario Human Rights Commission and Sports Canada, and she helped the Canadian Amateur Hockey Association establish a national women's championship.

Since 1983, female hockey players from each province have competed annually for women's hockey's top honour: the Abby Hoffman Cup.

The End of the Original Six Era

With just six teams, the NHL was an intense and exciting league. Players from all of the teams competed regularly, so they knew each other well. Rivalries both on and off the ice were fuelled by personal relationships as well as team spirit.

The small size of the league had its downside, though. Fans came from a relatively small part of North America — the Northeast and Midwest. Meanwhile, other sports were growing in popularity, especially baseball and football. They were competing for the loyalty — and dollars — of sports fans. Television networks were striking major deals with the sports leagues that could deliver fans across the continent.

NHL team owners had been reluctant to expand and share their profits for years. Now they realized it was grow or die. In 1967, the NHL announced it would double the

league's size. Six new teams would be allowed to join —
for a fee of $2 million each!

"When I was a kid," Don Cherry once recalled, "I used to pray to the Lord to make me a hockey player. I forgot to mention the NHL, and so I spent 16 years in the minors!"

The 1967 expansion teams were

- California Seals
- Los Angeles Kings
- Philadelphia Flyers
- Pittsburgh Penguins
- Minnesota North Stars
- St. Louis Blues

The original six teams were grouped together to become the East Division. The six new expansion teams became the West Division. The winner of each division would play at the end of the regular season for the Stanley Cup.

The Expansion Era Takes Off

At first, people didn't expect much from the expansion teams. But everyone was surprised by how well they did right off the bat. The new teams were scoring goals and drawing fans just like the established ones. Flyers manager Bud Poile felt secure enough to gloat: "This game has really arrived in Philadelphia. The fans have started to boo us and the refs."

GAME HIGHLIGHT

In the fall of 1968, defenceman Bill Sutherland was excited to play his first game for the expansion team, the Philadelphia Flyers. When he arrived at the rink, the security staff wouldn't let him in.

"But I'm playing tonight," he said. "I'm a Flyer!"

The attendant at the gate snapped, "Prove it!" But Sutherland couldn't. He was told to get lost since "Nobody gets in without a ticket!"

Sutherland was understandably ticked. He had to sneak into the arena when the guard was busy with "real" ticket holders! Later, as he skated onto the ice, he vowed to do something to make himself famous in Philly. He wound up scoring the first and only goal of the game!

Expansion brought several major changes to the game. First and foremost, the total number of games played each season jumped from 210 to 444.

Another change had to do with cold, hard cash. More games plus more ticket-buying fans equalled more money for the team owners. As more money flowed, the players began demanding bigger paycheques. They were able to get it, too, partly because their labour union, the National Hockey League Players' Association, was formed in 1967.

The union helped players negotiate with team management. It shifted the balance of power between owners and players.

Another exciting change was that there was more goal-scoring — tons of it! Stan Mikita's curved stick played a part. Some exceptional new players, like Phil Esposito and Bobby Orr, also had a big impact.

PROFILES IN HOCKEY

BOBBY ORR

"There were stars, superstars and then there's Bobby Orr."
— *Derek Sanderson*

Bobby Orr is considered by almost everyone to be one of the all-time greatest players of the great game. He was scouted by the pros when he was just 12 years old. The Boston Bruins decided to sponsor Orr's Bantam team then and there, so they could sign Orr when he was old enough.

Still only in grade 8, Orr began playing junior hockey for the Bruins' farm team, the OHL's Oshawa Generals. Even though he was just 14, he was named to the Second All-Star Team! The next three years in a row, he made the OHL's First All-Star Team.

Orr moved up to the NHL in 1966 when he turned 18 (he wasn't allowed to go pro before he came of age). With Orr as their secret weapon, the Bruins were able to turn their fortunes around. In 1968, the Bruins made the play-offs for the first time in nine years! They won the Stanley Cup in 1970 — their first in 29 years — thanks to Orr's incredible stickhandling.

For Orr, it was a dream come true. He said, "This is what every kid dreams of, scoring the winning goal in a Stanley Cup overtime final. Wow! I can't find words to express what I feel."

Bobby Orr received many honours, including two Stanley Cups, the Norris Trophy for best defenceman eight years in a row, and MVP three times. But perhaps the most memorable achievement of all was in 1971-72, when he became the first NHL player to receive a contract worth over $1 million!

While Bobby continued to dominate the ice, he was plagued by recurring knee problems. In 1976, he was only well enough to play 10 games. He became a free agent and signed with the Chicago Blackhawks. He retired in 1978, at only 30 years old, unable to play because of his shaky knees. How much greater would his legacy have been if his knees had held up? No one can say for sure; we can only tip our hats to a true hockey hero who changed the game forever.

Third Period:
The Modern Era Begins

THE SUMMIT SERIES

"When I saw it go in, I just went bonkers."
— *Paul Henderson*

The world changed completely for Canada and for hockey in 1972. That's when a team composed of the best players from all the NHL teams challenged the Soviet National team in an exhibition match called the Summit Series.

At that time, professional hockey players were forbidden to play in the Olympics. That meant that some of the greatest players of all time were banned from international competition at the highest levels. The solution? A separate series, for "fun" only.

But there was much more at stake, really, than good clean fun. For Canada, hockey was an unmatched source of pride. According to Harry Sinden, coach for Team Canada, there were only two things at which Canada ranked first in the world: "hockey and wheat."

But even more important, in 1972 the world was still locked in the Cold War — a stalemate between the world's two nuclear superpowers, the United States and the USSR. Canadians sided with their American allies, and the Soviet Union was the much-hated enemy. The hockey rink, therefore, became a substitute battlefield. The possibility of losing was simply unthinkable.

The first four games of the eight-game series were held in Canada, at four different arenas across the country: the Montreal Forum, Maple Leaf Gardens, Winnipeg Arena and Vancouver's Pacific Coliseum. The remaining four games were all played in Moscow at the Luzhniki Ice Palace.

The crowd went wild when Phil Esposito scored for Canada just 30 seconds into game 1. Canada scored again six minutes later, but the Soviets came back to tie the score by the end of the first period.

In the second period, Valeri Kharlamov scored twice for the Soviets, putting them in the lead 4–2. Bobby Clarke scored one more time, but the Soviets still managed to put away three more goals and take game one with a devastating score of 7–3.

Game 2 showed Team Canada's ability to grit its teeth and bear down even after a severe blow. In the third period, Canada was up by one, when Pete Mahovlich scored a short-handed goal to make the score 3–1 in favour of Canada! In the end, Canada took the game 4–1.

Game 3 ended in a 4–4 tie, despite Canada holding commanding leads at several points of the game.

But it was Game 4 that brought Team Canada and the nation to despair. Canada played badly and lost 5–3. Frustrated fans booed them off the ice!

Two weeks later, the Soviets and Canadians met again in Moscow for the second half of the series. In game 5, Canada lost again, 5–4! The loss put Team Canada in a *dicey* position. They *had* to win all of the remaining games!

Game 6 was a rough one. In the second period, Canadian Bobby Clarke broke Valeri Kharlamov's ankle with a deliberately hard slash of his stick. The Canadians ended up with 31 penalty minutes during the game! The Soviets, meanwhile, were only given 4, leading Team Canada to complain that the refs were biased. Canada won 3–2, but there were now hard feelings on both sides.

The animosity came out clearly in Game 7. The USSR's Boris Mikhailov commited a real no-no when he kicked Canada's Gary Bergman twice with the blade of his skate! Nevertheless, Canada won 4–3, on a late-third period goal by Paul Henderson.

Game 8 and the series came down to this: one final do-or-die match on Soviet ice. In Canada, the entire country shut down! Offices closed for the afternoon and schools brought in TVs so teachers and children could watch the game in the school gym or auditorium!

As the first period ended, the score was 2–2. But in the second period, the Soviets pulled ahead 5–3!

With things looking grim, Canada tied it up in the third period on goals by Phil Esposito and Yvan Cournoyer. The momentum shifted in Canada's favour!

In the final minute of play, Paul Henderson was on the bench. He jumped to his feet and called to Mahovlich to get off the ice. Henderson just knew he had to get in there: "I had this strange feeling that I could score the winning goal," he later recalled.

With 34 seconds left in the game, Henderson hit the ice. He described what happened next in the book *Team Canada 1972: Where Are They Now?*:

> "I was tripped up and crashed into the boards behind the net. I leaped up and moved in front, just in time to see Esposito take a shot at Tretiak from inside the faceoff circle. The rebound came right to my stick and I tried to slide the puck past Tretiak . . . He got a piece of it. But a second rebound came right to me. This time I flipped the puck over him and into the net."

That incredible rebound came to be known as "the goal heard around the world." It's perhaps the most famous goal in hockey history. With that one shot, Team Canada won the game and series, securing its place in hockey history for all time.

Fallout from the Summit Series

Although Canada wound up beating the Soviets in the Summit Series, the games left Team Canada badly shaken. They realized that the Soviets and other international teams were really, really good. They were better trained, more physically fit, and had skills that serious challenged Canada's dominance of the sport.

As a result, hockey began to be played differently in North America. International matches became more common, and many NHL teams began to adopt the Soviets' tougher training methods. When the USSR collapsed, many Soviet players signed with the NHL. Today, international players on NHL teams bring a wide range of talent to a formerly closed and insular sport.

PROFILES IN HOCKEY

PHIL ESPOSITO

Phil Esposito was a huge star for the Boston Bruins during the 1960s and 1970s. He scored 40+ goals seven years in a row and 50+ five years in a row! On his first year on the team, the Bruins made the playoffs. In his second year, they made the semi-finals. And in just his third year, the Bruins won the Stanley Cup!

Esposito loved hockey so much that his father had often said Phil would probably play the game for nothing. One day Phil shot back, "Dad you're right, and I have played for nothing, so I need to borrow some money!"

No wonder Esposito quickly developed a reputation

as a character and a practical joker. He was also super-stitious. Once, when he had a cold, he wore a turtleneck during a game. He scored a hat trick! He wore turtlenecks for every game after that!

During the 1975–1976 season, when his best days with the Bruins were behind him, Esposito was called to a meeting with Bruins coach Don Cherry. He was told he was going to be traded. "Okay," Esposito sighed, "but if you say [I'm going to the] New York [Rangers], I'm going to jump out that window." Cherry turned to his assistant and sadly said, "Open the window."

Esposito played for the Rangers until 1981, then stayed on as Assistant Coach. He later served as vice-president and general manager of the Rangers and the Tampa Bay Lightning.

GAME HIGHLIGHT

One of the highlights of Esposito's career was playing on Team Canada with his brother in the Summit Series. He was the Canadians' top individual scorer with seven goals and six assists.

THE LEAGUE EXPANDS AGAIN

In the 1970s, the NHL kept expanding. In 1970–1971, the Buffalo Sabres and Vancouver Canucks joined the league. In 1972–1973, two more teams came on board: the Atlanta Flames and the New York Islanders. In 1974–1975, the Kansas City Scouts and the Washington Capitals brought the number of teams in the NHL to 18.

In 1971, the Detroit Red Wings were totally humiliated by the Maple Leafs in a 13–0 shutout. After the game, embarrassed team captain Alex Delvecchio joked, "It would have been worse if we hadn't blocked the kick after Toronto's second touchdown!"

As the NHL grew, it attracted new fans all across the continent. But not everyone was satisfied with the level of play or the opportunity the league offered to players.

Watch Out — Here Comes the WHA

In 1971, two sharp sports promoters, Dennis Murphy and Gary Davidson, decided to form a rival league. They knew that many NHL stars were unhappy. The average salary for a NHL hockey player in 1972 was just $25,000, by far the lowest salary in any of the major sports. Furthermore, a clause in their employment contracts tied them to a team for life, even if they were offered a better deal elsewhere.

The league Murphy and Davidson founded was called the World Hockey Association (WHA). It promised higher salaries than the NHL and got rid of the hated "reserve clause."

The first season, featuring twelve teams, was scheduled to begin play in 1972. Would players — and fans — go for the new league? It wasn't a sure thing. After all, the NHL had long been *the* league for hockey. Who would want to take a chance on an unproven upstart?

Bobby Hull, for one. The incredibly popular Blackhawks star jumped to the WHA when he was offered a mind-boggling $2.7 million contract with the brand new Winnipeg Jets! Other big stars followed, and before long, the new league was off the ground.

The WHA presented a huge challenge to the NHL. No wonder the NHL did all it could to stop the new league in its tracks, like taking its owners to court. It even filed court orders against players like Bobby Hull to keep them from leaving the NHL!

In November 1972, a judge ruled against the NHL. The players were free to go the WHA if they chose.

GAME HIGHLIGHTS

The first WHA games were held on October 11, 1972. The Alberta Oilers defeated the Ottawa Nationals 7-4, and the Quebec Nordiques beat the Cleveland Crusaders 2-0.

WHA' Happened Next?

The new WHA struggled from the get-go. Many teams had financial troubles which never let up. The Miami Screaming Eagles, for example, screamed to a halt before they even played a single game! Other teams wound up hopping from city to city, trying to find enough paying fans. The Dayton Aeros flew to Houston, and the San Francisco Sharks cruised into Quebec as the Nordiques.

The New York Raiders, meanwhile, found themselves forced to share Madison Square Garden with the Rangers. A similar situation had proved disastrous once before, for the New York Americans, and the Raiders fared no better. They lasted less than half a season in New York City. Three new names and cities later, the team disbanded in 1977.

BALLARD BULLIES THE TOROS

When the WHA's Toronto Toros (formerly the Ottawa Nationals) played their first game in Maple Leaf Gardens, it was so dim they could hardly see! The Gardens' owner, Harold Ballard (who also owned the NHL's Leafs), demanded the Toros pay $3500 per game just to have the lights turned on! Toros' players also discovered that Ballard had taken away the pillows from the home team's bench. "Let 'em buy their own cushions!" he'd sniffed!

By 1976, many of the WHA's teams were on the verge of collapse. The league began discussing a merger with the NHL in 1977.

No progress was made, however, until 1979. By then, there were only six surviving WHA teams: the Edmonton Oilers, Hartford Whalers, Quebec Nordiques, Winnipeg Jets, Cincinnati Stingers and Birmingham Bulls. The first four joined the NHL. The Stingers and Bulls folded. The new NHL now had 21 teams, 6 of them in Canada.

One of the new NHL teams, the Edmonton Oilers, was to really shake up the league. On its roster was a rookie phenom by the name of Wayne Gretzky.

To make room for more seats in Maple Leaf Gardens, Ballard once had a large portrait of the Queen removed. His justification? "She doesn't pay me, I pay her. Besides, what the h— position can a queen play?" Of course, no one ever accused Harold Ballard of being a nice guy. In fact, he was a complete crook! In 1971, Ballard was convicted on 47 charges of fraud, theft and tax evasion and was sentenced to 9 years in a federal penitentiary!

TEST YOUR HOCKEY HISTORY KNOWLEDGE

1. The 1979 NHL–WHA merger owed its success to what beverage?
   a. Coffee
   b. Tea
   c. Beer

2. In 1979, Islander Billy Smith became the first goalie in NHL history to do what?
   a. Play in 500 games straight
   b. Score a goal
   c. Wear a decorated mask

3. In 1976, Maple Leafs coach Red Kelly installed pyramids in the players' dressing room. Why?
   a. He was born in Egypt.
   b. He was superstitious, and believed that doing so would harness "pyramid power" for the team.
   c. The pyramids were actually ice chests in an innovative new shape.

4. During a game, St. Louis Blues player George Morrison got really, really hungry. What did he do?
   a. He left the arena to grab a sandwich, causing his team to forfeit the game.
   b. He grabbed a hot dog during intermission and brought it out on the ice with him. He ate it on the ice and the rink wound up decorated with mustard and relish!
   c. Took out a cell phone and ordered a pizza — to be delivered to him on the ice.

5. In 1984, Canadian astronaut Marc Garneau did what?

    a. Took a hockey puck and stick along for the ride on his first space voyage!

    b. Broadcast his Stanley Cup winner prediction from the space shuttle.

    c. Played goalie for the Maple Leafs for one period.

6. You're watching hockey and you rub your eyes as two jerseys marked "Sutter" whiz across the screen. Think you're seeing double? Wait — there's another one! And another! *Just how many hockey players named Sutter were there anyway?*

    a. 5

    b. 6

    c. 4

7. When did the NHL introduce sudden death overtime?

    a. 1946

    b. 1969

    c. 1983

Turn the page for answers.

ANSWERS

1. c. When negotiations began between the NHL and WHA, the owners of the Canadiens opposed the deal. They believed adding Canadian teams would hurt their profits. Fans in Quebec City, Edmonton and Winnipeg were outraged. They badly wanted their teams to survive. So they came up with a clever plan — they initiated a national boycott of Molson, a beer company. Why? Because Molson also owned the Canadiens!

   With beer sales tanking across the country, Molson caved. They signed the merger deal in March, 1979.

2. b.

3. c.

4. b.

5. a.

6. b. During the 1980s, six brothers from the Sutter family all played hockey for the NHL. During one memorable 1983 Islanders-Flyers game, four of the brothers were on the ice at the same time!

7. c. The 1983–1984 season. Since 1942, all NHL games had ended when regulation time ran out, no matter what the score. Unfortunately, that meant many games ended unsatisfyingly in ties.

The addition of a five minute overtime period made for more exciting hockey. The first team to score in that five minutes became the automatic winner and the game came to an end. (The shortest overtime ever played was just nine seconds long!) If no goals were scored during the five minute extra period, however, the game could still end in a tie.

The NHL played under these overtime rules until the 2005–2006 season when the shootout was introduced.

HOCKEY, EIGHTIES STYLE

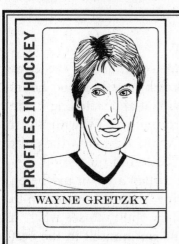

PROFILES IN HOCKEY

WAYNE GRETZKY

You can't talk about hockey in the 1980s without talking about Wayne Gretzky. As one of the all-time best players to ever take to the ice, he dominated the game in a way no one has before or since.

Gretzky's incredible talent was obvious from early in his childhood. At 6 years of age, he was already beating the pants off 10-year-olds. At just 11, he was already a star — signing autographs and taking phone calls from national magazines. That's because he had racked up 378 goals in just 69 games (that's more than 5 goals in every game he played)! No wonder he was already being heralded as "The Great One."

Wayne's Childhood World

Gretzky's parents always supported him in his love of hockey. His dad, Wally, even built a rink for Wayne in the backyard which everyone called "Wally's Coliseum"!

In his autobiography, Gretzky describes his childhood passion for hockey: "All I wanted to do in the winters was be on the ice. I'd get up in the morning, skate from 7:00 to 8:30, go to school, come home at 3:30, stay on the ice until my mom insisted I come in for dinner, eat in my skates, then go back out until 9:00. On Saturdays and Sundays we'd have huge games, but nighttime became my time. It was a sort of unwritten rule around the neighbourhood that I was to be out there myself or with my dad."

What Made Gretzky So Good?

Wayne's dedication to the game continued off the ice as well. When he was a kid, Gretzky would spend hours studying the game, both playing it and watching it. He says, "I would sit down in front of the TV with a pen and I'd watch the puck on TV and I'd follow the puck for the whole period . . . At the end of the period, you would see heavy lines in one certain area, or maybe on one end if a team is dominating." His determination to learn helped build his legendary ability to see where a play was going to happen, and put himself in the best position to capitalize on it.

At 14, Gretzky began playing Junior B hockey with the Vaughan Nationals. That year, he was named Rookie of the Year in the Metro Junior B Hockey League, scoring 60 points in just 28 games.

"Some guys play hockey. Gretzky plays 40 mph chess." – Lowell Cohn

Magic Number 99

Everyone agreed Gretzky had great hockey skills. But they also agreed his small size was a handicap. Scouts wrote about him, "Too small, too slow," and "Won't survive the rough play." He was so slender, an observer joked, "he could wear a fur coat on Halloween — and go out disguised as a pipe cleaner."

Gretzky showed everyone, though, that size isn't everything.

Wayne Goes WHA

In 1978, the NHL did not allow players under the age of 18 to sign. Wayne was just 17, but was more than ready for the big leagues. What would he do?

One option was to go to the rival pro league, the WHA. They didn't care if Gretzky was 17 or 77! Gretzky signed a 7-year contract with the WHA's Indianapolis Racers — a contract worth $1.75 million US!

The new teenage millionaire only played eight games for the Racers. The team was in financial trouble, so they moved Gretzky to the Edmonton Oilers. On Gretzky's 18th birthday, he signed a 21-year contract — worth $21 million — with the owner of the Oilers.

The Golden Years

When the WHA merged with the NHL, Gretzky finally had the chance to play with the best players of his generation, in a strong, established league.

And wow, did he play. From 1979 to 1988, the Oilers made the playoffs every single year and won the Stanley Cup 4 times, largely due to Gretzky's incredible talent. He captained the team from 1983 to 1988, supported by other legendary players including Mark Messier, Glenn Anderson, Jari Kurri, Paul Coffey and Grant Fuhr. Together, they formed a powerhouse dynasty for the record books.

The Royal Wedding

Then Wayne fell in love.

He met actress Janet Jones, and in 1988 they were married in a ceremony that was the highlight of the Canadian social season. The event was reported to have cost over a million dollars!

The "royal wedding," was more than just a romantic

love-fest, though. It signalled the start of a new era in Gretzky's career. He naturally wanted to spend as much time as possible with his new bride. Her career as an actress kept her in Hollywood. The Oilers, alas, were based thousands of kilometres away in Alberta.

At the same time, Oilers' owner Peter Pocklington was suffering from money troubles. Wayne Gretzky was by far the highest-priced player on the team. It made sense, then, for the Oilers to trade Wayne to the Los Angeles Kings, solving Pocklington's money woes and Gretzky's love pangs in one fell swoop.

Unless, of course, you were a red-blooded Canadian!

"The Trade" was greeted with horror and outrage across the nation. How could Canada's own home-grown hockey hero be traded to an American team? Politicians urged the Canadian government to block the deal. An effigy of Peter Pocklington was burned on the steps of Edmonton's Northlands Coliseum! Nevertheless, on August 9, 1988, Gretzky became Gretz-King.

The Great One in L.A.

In his first season with the Kings, Gretzky led the team to a second place finish in their division.

GAME HIGHLIGHT
LA Kings goon Randy Holt once earned a record 67 penalty minutes — in a 60-minute game!

In 1993, the Kings at last made it to the Stanley Cup finals, the first time in the franchise's history. They lost to the Canadiens, but even so, the season was considered a big success. Kings tickets were the hottest draw in town, and their games were frequently sold out. Gretzky had brought ice hockey to the Southwest and made it hot!

"Trying to stop Wayne is like throwing a blanket over a ghost." – Kings' head coach Parker MacDonald

Moving on to Greener Pastures

In 1996, Gretzky was traded to the St. Louis Blues. He played one season there before heading to New York City to play for the Rangers. In 1999, number 99 retired from professional hockey.

No other player has captured the hearts and minds of hockey fans to the degree of Wayne Gretzky. As a boy, he looked up to hockey legend Gordie Howe. For kids today, Wayne Gretzky still stands above others as The Great One — the hockey player who changed the game forever with his skill, intelligence and indomitable spirit.

Here are some of the 60 records Wayne Gretzky set during his 1,487-game career (as of the day he retired from hockey).

Some of the NHL Records Held by Wayne Gretzky	
Most regular season goals	894
Most goals, including playoffs	1,016
Most goals, one season	92
Most regular season assists	1,963
Most assists, including playoffs	2,223
Most assists, one season	163
Most assists, one game	7 (tied with Billy "The Kid" Taylor) — 3 separate times!
Most regular season points	2,857
Highest goals-per-game average, one season	1.18
Highest assists-per-game average, career (300+ games)	1.321
Most 100-or-more point seasons	15
Most three-goal games, one season	10 (twice!)
Most playoff goals, career	122
He also won the following awards:	
The Hart Trophy – 9 times	
Art Ross Trophy – 10 times	
Conn Smythe Trophy – 2 times	
Lester B. Pearson Award – 5 times	

The Miracle on Ice

The 1972 Summit Series had been a larger than life match for Canada. Eight years later, another international hockey match became just as a big a deal for the United States. It came to be known as the Miracle on Ice.

In 1980, an Olympic year, the best hockey team in the world was still the Soviets. Team USA, on the other hand, was mostly made up of university students (NHLers *still* couldn't play in the Olympics).

No one expected very much from the American college kids, but they had a secret weapon — a very determined coach, Herb Brooks. Instead of accepting defeat, he gathered the best college players from around the United States. He taught them how to work together, and he made them focus on speed, fitness and discipline — just like the Soviets. Even so, their chances were rated at between zero and nil.

At the Olympics, Team USA started off with a 2–2 tie against Sweden. Then they racked up wins over Czechoslovakia, Norway, Romania and West Germany. They were on fire! People started saying the young Yanks might go all the way!

It was definitely a piece of bad luck, then, when they discovered who they'd be facing in their first medal round. You guessed it — the USSR.

At the start of the game, the Soviets came out like gang-busters. They pummelled the Americans, outshooting them by a huge margin. The US was down 2–1 at the end of the first period. But then Dave Christian took a long shot that rebounded. Forward Mark Johnson nabbed it and scored at the buzzer! Team USA had tied it up!

The game stayed close through the second period. Tensions reached an all-time high when the Soviets scored to take the lead, 3–2. But in the third period, the Americans tied it up again on a power-play goal.

The noise in the Lake Placid, NY arena was deafening. Then, with 10 minutes left in the game, American team captain Mike Eruzione scored on a 8.5-metre wrist shot! USA 4 – USSR 3!

Could the Americans hold off the Russians for ten more minutes? The country held its breath. The clock ticked down:

> "Eleven seconds. You got ten seconds, the countdown going on right now. Five seconds left in the game! Do you believe in miracles? Yes!"
> –Broadcaster Al Michaels

Fans all over America went wild. Although Team USA still had to win one more game before claiming the gold medal, Americans felt like they'd already won it all. They'd beaten the unbeatable Soviets, their old nemesis on and off the ice! The "Miracle on Ice" would go down in history as one of the most spectacular and dramatic victories in hockey history.

Back at Home . . .
Why Are the Girls Still Missing from the Rink?

By 1980, more girls and women were playing hockey across North America than ever before. But they still faced huge hurdles. Boys' and men's hockey in Canada got tons more money, which meant better equipment and better training. The guys also got more ice time, so they had more opportunity to build skills. Twenty-five years after Abby Hoffman had been shut out of competitive hockey, not much had changed for Canadian girls. They still got the short end of the (hockey) stick.

In 1981, another 10-year-old girl, just like Abby Hoffman, wanted to play hockey. Also like Abby, she wanted to compete at the highest level available — the boys' Metro Toronto Hockey League. Her name was Justine Blainey.

Justine filed a discrimination complaint with the Human Rights Commission. The commission told her to get lost! That's because back in 1981, the Ontario Human Rights Code specifically *allowed* sexual discrimination in sports!

But Justine didn't give up. A new Charter of Rights and Freedoms had just been established in Canada. She decided to use it to challenge the Ontario Human Rights Code itself!

It took four years before Justine Blainey's case was finally heard in the Supreme Court of Canada. Finally, in 1985, the Canadian Supreme Court gave Justine the victory she, and all girls, deserved. They announced that the Ontario Human Rights Code was illegal, and that girls had the absolute right to compete on the ice with boys.

Justine won the battle Abby Hoffman had started twenty-five years earlier. Their courage and determination led the way for all Canadian girls and women who want to play competitive hockey at the top levels.

Here Come the Europeans!

In 1980, pro hockey in North America was still mainly played by Canadians and Americans. A few players from Europe, such as the Leafs' Swedish defenceman Borje Salming, started trickling into the NHL in the 1970s. But they were few and far between.

One reason was that the best European players were mostly from behind the "Iron Curtain" — countries under the control of the Soviet Union. The Soviet Union was a brutal totalitarian state. Most people who lived in its shadow were not ever allowed to leave their homelands. They had to sneak out, or *defect*, a high-risk, cloak-and-dagger project!

A few hockey players took the gamble. Peter Stastny played hockey for Czechoslovakia, a country "behind" the Iron Curtain. One day, he said something nasty about the Soviet regime. That was a real no-no! The backlash came right away: watch your tongue or you'll be kicked off the team!

The threat scared Stastny half to death. That's when he decided to leave, he said: "because they had total control and could manipulate you anyway they wanted, there was no future for me [in Czechoslovakia]."

When he was sent to an international tournament in Austria, he knew the moment had come. Secretly, late at night, Stastny, his wife and his brother Anton sneaked out of their hotel and hurried to the Innsbruck airport. A private plane was waiting for them. They boarded the plane, knowing they could probably never go back to Czechoslovakia.

Stastny's gamble paid off. Stastny wound up playing hockey for the Nordiques from 1980 to 1989. He was a top scorer and fan favourite. He and Anton were also able to ransom their brother Marian from Czechoslovakia for $30,000. They brought him to Canada too, where he also played for the Nordiques.

According to Stastny, defecting to Canada "was the best decision I ever made. It has given my family the choices and options that people behind the Iron Curtain could only dream of. Then, to play pro hockey with my two brothers was like icing on the cake."

The Iron Curtain Melts

With the Stastnys safe in Canada, the trickle of players from behind the Iron Curtain grew to a flood. In 1989, the first player from the Soviet Union itself, Alexander Mogilny, defected after a tournament in Sweden. The story became front page news all over the world, partly because it signalled that the USSR was losing its grip. In fact, the country fell apart just two years later.

Free to travel, many more Russian and European players came to the NHL.

GAME HIGHLIGHT
In 1979, less than 5% of players drafted to the NHL hailed from Europe. By 2000, that figure had risen to 42%!

The international players helped improve hockey in the NHL. New talent and different styles of play made for more exciting and less predictable action.

THE NINETIES

As the century that made hockey the game it is today came to a close, there were still some changes in the wind . . .

The Quack Heard Round the World —
The Mighty Ducks Join the League

Gretzky's success in Los Angeles had proven that there was room for professional hockey in places not usually considered to be "hockey country." So the league began expanding again in 1991, bringing new blood to an organization that had just reached its 75th birthday.

The first team to come on-stream was the San Jose Sharks. The following year, the Ottawa Senators and the Tampa Bay Lightning signed on. And in 1993, the Mighty Ducks of Anaheim and the Florida Panthers joined the growing NHL menagerie.

The Mighty Ducks were owned by the Walt Disney Company, and had been named after a team portrayed in a 1992 Disney movie called — uh-huh — *The Mighty Ducks*.

BARBECUED WINGS?

The Ducks' mascot is a giant quacker called "Wild Wing." During home games, he flies into the arena suspended from the rafters. Once, the rigging malfunctioned, and the unlucky duck was left dangling fifteen metres above the ice! Another time, the birdbrain attempted to jump through a wall of flame. He fell short and accidentally set himself on fire!

The Disney-owned team got lots of publicity. But it wasn't the only new team to get plenty of press during the 1990s. The Tampa Bay Lightning electrified fans by signing the first woman to ever play in the league!

The Girls Get in the Game

Many thought Tampa Bay hired Manon Rhéaume just to get publicity. But Rhéaume was a talented hockey player in her own right, with a career many NHL players may have envied.

In 1992, she was invited to the Lightning's training camp. She played in a pre-season game against the St. Louis Blues. Then, she signed a three-year contract with the Lightning's minor league affiliate, the Atlanta Knights.

On December 13, 1992, Rhéaume made history when she played in goal in a regular season game against the Salt Lake City Golden Eagles. It was the first time a woman had ever played in a men's professional hockey game!

Rhéaume wound up playing a total of 24 games for various men's minor league teams between 1992 and 1997. Her biggest successes, though, came in women's hockey. In 1992 and 1994, she received gold medals for Canada at the World Championships, and she won a silver medal at the Olympics in 1998.

GAME HIGHLIGHT

In 1991, the first official women's world hockey championships were held in Ottawa. Team Canada, wearing pink jerseys, won gold. The following year, the number of girls who registered to play league hockey jumped 40 per cent. Girls were finally getting their chance to enjoy the game of hockey, just like the boys.

In 1999, more than 100 years after the first women's hockey games were played in Canada, a national, professional league for women's hockey was finally established. The National Women's Hockey League (NWHL) had ten teams. It merged in 2007 with the Canadian Women's Hockey League (CWHL), which currently operates with six teams in Ontario and Quebec.

MARIO LEMIEUX

He was the only player in the '90s who really challenged Gretzky's celebrity status: Mario Lemieux, the Pittsburgh Penguin forward everyone called "Super Mario." Lemieux began playing hockey at age 3 in his basement with his brothers. They used wooden spoons as hockey sticks and bottle caps for the pucks.

According to family legend, Mario Lemieux's father would sometimes bring snow into the living room and pack it down, so the kids could play hockey indoors after dark!

At 15, Mario was drafted by a Quebec Junior team, the Laval Voisins. In 1983–1984, he broke the league record for most points scored in a season with 282 in just 70 games.

In 1984, Mario signed with the Pittsburgh Penguins. In his first game in the NHL, he scored his first goal on his first shot! Later that season, he became the first rookie to be named MVP in the NHL All-Star game. In 1988, he surpassed Gretzky as the year's top scorer for the first time, to snag the Art Ross trophy. He also won his very first Hart Trophy for being the league's Most Valuable Player, and collected his second All-Star Game MVP award after he set a record by scoring six points in the game.

Through the rest of the 1980s and early 1990s, Lemieux battled with Gretzky for top honours and set many records and personal bests. One astonishing coup happened on December 31, 1988. Lemieux became the only player in NHL history to score in all five possible ways in one game: even-strength, power-play, shorthanded, penalty shot, and empty-net!

In 1991 and 1992, Lemieux led the Penguins to the Stanley Cup. But in 1993, Super Mario's career came to a shocking halt. He was diagnosed with a potentially deadly form of cancer called Hodgkin's lymphoma. He was forced to take time off from the Penguins to undergo radiation treatments.

When he returned two months later, weakened from radiation treatments and still plagued by a recurring back injury, he still managed to score a goal and an assist against the Philadelphia Flyers. He was given a standing ovation by Philadelphia fans, a rare gesture of support for a rival team's player.

With Lemieux back on the roster, the struggling Penguins turned their fortunes around. They had a record-setting winning streak of 17 games, and finished first in the league for the first time in the team's history.

At the end of the 1993 season, Super Mario underwent surgery on his back. He played during 1993–1994, but worn out from his on-going cancer treatments, he decided not to play in 1994–1995. Back again in 1995–1996, he scored his 500th career goal and led the league in scoring.

Lemieux decided to retire in 1997. The Hockey Hall of Fame acknowledge the extraordinary nature of Lemieux's hockey achievements and decided to waive the waiting period before a player could be inducted; Lemieux was inducted that Fall.

You Can't Keep Super Mario Down!

Mario didn't like retirement. After three years on the sidelines, he made a surprise comeback for the 2000–2001 season. He still had the old Super Mario magic, getting an assist only 33 seconds into his first shift!

In 2006, Lemieux was 40 years old and plagued by recurring injuries. On January 24, Mario Lemieux announced his second retirement. But even so, he had no intention of leaving hockey behind. His plans included continuing on as a team owner! Lemieux had become majority owner of the Penguins in 1999, after the team declared bankruptcy.

Mario Lemieux had a staggeringly successful career, despite the fact that his illnesses and injuries severely limited his time on the ice. Many believe he would have overtaken Wayne Gretzky in many more areas if he'd had better health. Nevertheless, Super Mario, the "Magnificent One," has more than earned his place in the pantheon of hockey greats.

A NEW MILLENNIUM
It was December 31, 1999. The whole world held its breath as the clock ticked down to a new millennium — the dawning of Y2K, the year 2000.

No one knew what changes the momentous event would bring, but one thing was guaranteed: change was definitely coming.

In the world of hockey, those changes would be both good and bad.

The 2002 Olympics
Heading into the 2002 Olympics in Salt Lake City, Team Canada had a huge obstacle to overcome: they hadn't won a gold medal in hockey at the Olympics in 50 years. Hockey Canada resolved that 2002 would be the year to break that losing streak.

The 1998 Olympic games were the first in which NHL players were allowed to participate. Since most of the NHLers were inexperienced in the Olympic format, both the American and Canadian teams failed to medal.

Four years later, both teams were now ready to rumble.

Wayne Gretzky was brought in to manage Team Canada. "Magnificent" Mario Lemieux was appointed team captain. Other NHL stars such as Eric Lindros, Martin Brodeur, Curtis Joseph, Mike Peca and Joe Sakic rounded out Team Canada.

The United States also had some great players on their roster: Gary Suter, Brian Rafalski and Brett Hull. The team was heavy on veterans, though, like the '67 Leafs, and no one expected them to win.

Of course, the Russians were still a hockey powerhouse, with the most experience of all three teams in International play. Even so, Canada was expected to bring home Olympic gold for the first time in generations.

Canada's Path to Gold

Canada's first game was against Sweden. Team Canada lost, 5–2! "Getting smoked by Sweden probably was a good thing, because we knew we had to get better," Joe Sakic told *Sports Illustrated*.

The loss put a huge amount of pressure on team manager Wayne Gretzky. The pressure didn't ease up after their second game against Germany, either. It was a squeaker. Canada scraped out a 3–2 win, but now the grumblings against Gretzky were starting to sound like growls. They got even louder when Canada's next game, against the Czech Republic, ended in a tie.

Luckily, Canada found its rhythm just in time. They

handily beat Finland 2–1 in the quarter-final, then demolished Belarus 7–1.

It had been a difficult and painful path, but Canada had made it to the final round. Now, they'd be playing Team USA for the gold.

Mario Makes His Move

Mario Lemieux made an astonishing play early in the first period that may have sealed the game for the Canadians. Defenceman Chris Pronger fired a pass across the zone. Lemieux faked that he received the pass and took a "shot" on net. The goalie lunged in Lemieux's direction, leaving the net open for Paul Kariya, who had picked up the pass behind Lemieux! This brilliant play allowed Canada to tie the game and come back in the next period to take the lead.

Gretzky's Good Luck Charm

No one really knows how the idea got started, or who was behind it. But somehow, Canada's fortunes were given a boost by an unlikely good luck charm: a Canadian loonie.

Trent Evans was the icemaker at the Salt Lake arena. He also happened to be Canadian. And somehow, under his watchful eye, but unknown to any one else, a loonie was buried at centre ice!

Did this Lucky Loonie help Team Canada during that gold medal game? No one knows for sure. What we do know, though, is that the 2002 Olympic final was one of the most exciting, and most watched, hockey games ever until that time. We also know that Canada's men's *and* women's hockey teams won gold in Salt Lake!

Great Games in Hockey History —

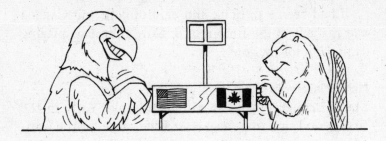

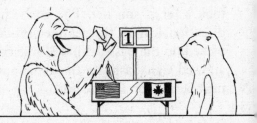

The first goal of the game is scored by Tony Amonte for the United States on a breakaway.

Then Paul Kariya and Jarome Iginla score for Canada, less than four minutes apart in the first period, seizing the lead.

In the second period, the momentum seems to shift to the Americans.

Team Canada vs. Team USA

Brian Rafalski grabs the puck during a US power play opportunity and scores, tying up the game.

American Jeremy Roenick draws a tripping penalty. Joe Sakic scores on the power play, putting Canada back into the lead.

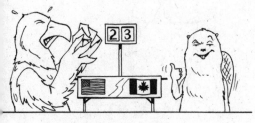

In the third period, with just four minutes to play, Steve Yzerman shoots from the left point. Iginla redirects it toward the net ... Score! 4-2 Canada!

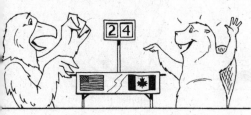

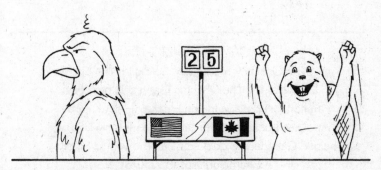

Sakic then slips in his second goal of the game. With a score of 5-2, Team Canada wins Olympic gold!

GAME HIGHLIGHT
Wayne Gretzky made sure to dig up the Lucky
Loonie after the Olympic Games. It now has
an honoured place in the Hockey Hall of Fame.
Another Lucky Loonie, called the Helsinki Loonie,
helped Canada win gold again at the World Hockey
Championships in 2003!

Another Gold for Canada

The 2002 Olympics yielded another gold medal in hockey for Canada, this time from the women's team.

Team Canada owed much of its success to hockey legend Hayley Wickenheiser. She began playing top level hockey at the age of 15, when she was named to Canada's National Women's Team for the first time. She won her first gold medal in 1994 at the World Championship games in Lake Placid, NY. She followed it up with 5 golds and 4 silvers in 13 years of international play (she missed one year due to an injury).

At the 1998 Olympics, Wickenheiser helped bring a silver medal home to Canada and was named to the tournament's all-star team. Her performance was so strong that she was invited to participate in the Philadelphia Flyers' rookie camps in 1998 and 1999.

Bringing It Home

But it was at the 2002 Olympics that Wickenheiser's star began to shine most brightly. On the pre-Olympic tour, she played 15 games and scored 19 points. She was the top scorer, and named tournament MVP. The sweetest honour of all was wrestling the gold away from Canada's arch-rivals, the US Women's team. She went on to bring home two more gold Olympic medals, in 2006 and 2010!

Pro Play

In 2003, Wickenheiser joined a European men's hockey league to play professional hockey. She played for the Finnish team Salamat, and became the first woman to score a goal playing in a men's professional league. Wickenheiser has become a hockey hero across Canada, especially to girls, who consider her an inspiring role model. She was selected one of the Top 100 Most Influential People in Hockey by *The Hockey News*, one of the 25 Toughest Athletes by *Sports Illustrated* and one of the Top 50 Most Powerful Women in Canada by *The Globe and Mail.*

The Season that Never Was

The 2004–2005 season was the worst one ever for many hockey fans. That's because the NHL cancelled it entirely! It was all because of a dispute over money between the players and owners.

In 2004, the labour agreement between the NHLPA (the players' union) and the league owners expired. A new agreement had to be negotiated. Many teams in the NHL were having financial troubles. Players' salaries had more than tripled since the last labour agreement had been negotiated a decade before. Revenues for team owners, however, had not kept pace. That put an enormous amount of pressure on the team owners to try to keep their costs low and predictable. Setting up a salary cap was one way to achieve that goal.

The players didn't like that idea. They wanted to be able to earn as much as possible, and didn't wanted to be limited by an arbitrary top number.

While negotiations ground on, hockey went on hiatus. No NHL games were played throughout the fall. Many players went overseas to play in European leagues.

By January, it looked like the entire 2004–2005 season would have to be scrapped. But still, the two sides couldn't come to an agreement. On February 16, 2005, the NHL announced that there would be no hockey for the rest of the year. By doing so, they became the very first major sports league to cancel an entire season because of labour problems.

Nearly a whole year went by before the two sides came to an agreement. In July, 2005, the 310 day lockout finally came to an end.

When hockey resumed in the fall of 2005, it was to an uncertain future. No one was sure if the disappointed fans would come back. At many arenas, ticket prices were slashed to draw fans back. And all across the league, new rules were adopted to make the game more exciting.

Shootout Shenanigans

One of the rule changes really stirred the emotions of disgruntled hockey fans.

At issue was the ongoing problem of too many tied games. Sudden death overtime had been added in 1983 to reduce the problem. But there were still plenty of games that remained tied, even after the extra five minutes of play.

The NHL decided to adopt shootouts to eliminate ties once and for all.

2010 OLYMPICS

As the first decade of the 21st century drew to a close, Canadians geared up for the Winter Olympics to be held in Vancouver, BC. Team Canada's promise to "own the podium" was taken to heart all across the country. Canadian athletes, who had never won a gold medal for Canada on Canadian soil, were determined to end that drought.

Ladies First

The women's team headed into the Games as the reigning Olympic champs, having won gold at the previous two Olympic meets. But Team USA was ranked number one in the world, having won the previous two world championships.

Both teams were determined to win gold, but the numbers pointed to a Canadian victory. The Canadians were 6–1–1 against the Yanks in the lead-up to the games, and they had outscored them 28–14 in matchups since the previous October.

Team USA's path to the finals included games against China, Russia, Finland and Sweden. The Americans had two shutouts, against Russia and Finland, and allowed China and Sweden only 1 goal each. The Americans, on the other hand, put a total of 40 pucks into the net!

The gold-medal game was billed as a "Clash of the Titans." Team Canada's head coach, Melody Davidson, kept everyone on edge by keeping her choice of game goalie secret until the last moment!

Her choice for goaltender, Shannon Szabados, had played hockey on boys' teams her entire career. She was the first woman to play in one of Canada's top leagues, the Western Hockey League. Szabados had also played on the men's team at Grant MacEwan University in Edmonton.

In the first period, Canadian veteran Jennifer Botterill fed Marie-Philip Poulin a perfect pass in front of the net. Poulin buried it. Canada was on the board!

Then, with 3:10 left in the first period, Poulin scored again with a hard shot low to goalie Jessie Vetter's glove side. Team Canada was up 2–0!

Szabados killed every US drive, stopping 28 out of 28 shots on goal for a perfect game. Team Canada won gold over the US in a heart stopper of a shutout!

Next — The Men's Turn

The two-week long party that was the Vancouver Olympics had reached a fever pitch by the time the Canadian men's hockey team took to the ice for the gold-medal game. It had not been as easy a journey as the women's. Overconfidence almost saw them knocked out of the running in the preliminary rounds!

Early Games of the Tourney

As the nation watched the first round on television or on live computer feed, Team Canada skated to an easy victory over Norway, 8–0.

Game two against Switzerland promised to be another easy victory, but Team Canada was in for a shock. Despite outshooting the Swiss 47–23, the Canadians let a 2–0 lead slip away. Regulation time ended with the game tied, 2–2!

After five minutes of overtime failed to settle it, it all came down to a shootout. On his second attempt, Sidney Crosby fired in a wrist shot to win the game!

Even though Team Canada won, they were still in trouble. To guarantee a spot in the quarter finals, they'd have to win their next game. Otherwise, they'd be sent on the path to a longer qualification round.

Their next opponent, however was Team USA.

Canada vs. USA Part 1

Just 41 seconds into the game, Team USA took the first of three leads. Team Canada put the pressure on and managed to tie things up twice with goals from Eric Staal and Dany Heatley. But even after a goal by Sidney Crosby, the Canadians were never able to close the gap left by the Americans' final lead. The final score was 5–3. Team USA had trounced Team Canada on home ice. It was a humiliating loss for the team and the country.

Detour to the Finals

The stinging defeat by Team USA was shame enough for the Canadians. But there was a practical downside, too. Team Canada was now rerouted into an additional qualifying round before they could get back on the medal track. Their arch-enemy, Team USA, on the other hand, was passed straight through to the quarter-finals.

Team Canada's next game was against Germany. Luckily, it was a cakewalk: Jarome Iginla scored twice. Joe Thornton, Shea Weber, Sidney Crosby, Mike Richards, Scott Niedermayer and Rick Nash also scored, and Eric Staal racked up three assists for a final score of 8–2.

In the quarter-finals the next night, Canada faced their old enemy, Russia. Canadian goals came in a veritable blizzard during the first half of the game, and Canada took the win 7–3. A 3–2 win over Slovakia in the semis, and Canada was on to the big game.

The Big Game

Team USA had handily put down Switzerland in their quarter-final match, 2–0, then Finland, 6–1, preparing the ground for the showdown of the new century. It was Team Canada vs. Team USA for the gold and the glory.

Things got off to a strong start for Team Canada. By the end of the second period, they were 2–0 on goals by Jonathan Toews and Corey Perry.

But the Americans weren't about to give up gold without a fight. Ryan Kesler deflected a long wrist shot from his teammate Patrick Kane and scored!

Canada entered the third period up 2–1. Team USA

kept up the pressure, banging shot after shot toward goalie Roberto Luongo. The Canadian defence remained rock-solid. With just 24 seconds remaining, a shot by Patrick Kane caromed off of Jamie Langenbrunner's skate. Zack Parise came around the net, picked up the puck, tucked it in behind Luongo and tied the game!

The gasps of pain and shock from the crowd were ear-shattering. An entire country saw the gold slipping from their grasp.

Team Canada came back on the ice for a 20-minute, 4-on-4 overtime. As they had through the entire game, Canada dominated the play. And yet, they could not score.

At 7:40 into overtime, the puck found its way to Sidney Crosby. Crosby had disappointed fans by turning in a ho-hum offensive performance all through the games. But now, he had the chance to make everything right. Crosby took it. Working the boards like a veteran, he laid a pass off to Jarome Iginla and darted toward the goal. He left Brian Rafalski contemplating the snow in his skate path as he set up, in the clear, in front of the goal. The pass from Iginla was on the money. Crosby flicked it in. He had just won the gold medal for Canada!

SIDNEY CROSBY

First, there was Wayne Gretzky, "The Great One." Then came Sidney Crosby, "The Next One."

Crosby began his hockey "career" when he was just two years old. Still in diapers, he would shoot pucks at the washer and dryer in his family's basement until they were dented beyond repair!

He learned to skate at three, and thanks both to his natural talent and his father's coaching (his dad had played junior hockey and been drafted by the Montreal Canadiens, although he'd never played for them), he quickly became a star in his local league.

At the age of 14, Crosby began playing for the Dartmouth Subways in the Midget AAA league. He scored 217 regular season and playoff points for his team. The team's performance was good enough to earn them a spot at the national championship tournament, the Air Canada Cup.

During the tourney, Crosby's opponents often became frustrated when confronted by Crosby's superior talent on the ice. Some intentionally tried to hurt him! From the stands, parents taunted and even threatened him. In consequence, he decided not to wear his jersey between tourney games so he wouldn't be recognized!

Crosby's team wound up finishing the tournament in second place. Scoring 18 points in 5 games, he received both the MVP Award and the Top Scorer Award.

Partly because of his treatment at the tournament, Crosby decided to move to the US to attend Shattuck-Saint Mary's Boarding School in Minnesota. During the 2002–2003 season, Crosby led the Shattuck-Saint Mary's Sabres to the a US national championship.

The following year, Crosby was ready to move up. He was the first pick of the Rimouski Océanic of the Quebec Midget Junior Hockey League. By the end of his first season in the league, he had been named Player of the Year, Top Rookie, and Top Scorer — the first player in the league to earn all three honours at once.

In 2005, Crosby turned 18 and was ready to go pro. He was such a hot prospect that every NHL team wanted him. As a result, that year the NHL draft was given a tongue-in-cheek nickname: "The Sidney Crosby Sweepstakes." The winner? The Pittsburgh Penguins.

Crosby made his NHL debut with the Penguins in October 2005, and scored his first professional point (an assist) against the New Jersey Devils. He scored his first pro goal at the Penguins home opener a few days later, against the Boston Bruins.

The following year, Crosby leapt from being a promising rookie into the top tier of hockey greats. He became the first teenager to lead the NHL in scoring since Wayne Gretzky in 1980. Also in 2006, he became the youngest player in NHL history to win the Art Ross Trophy, and the youngest scoring champ in any major North American pro sport. In 2007, he was named Penguins' team captain, the youngest in NHL history. Later that year, he signed a new five year contract with the Penguins for $43.5 million! In 2009, he led the Penguins to the Stanley Cup, becoming the youngest team captain in NHL history to win the prize.

Post-game Analysis

The history of hockey in Canada has been a long and glorious one. But it just keeps getting better. Today, more kids than ever are playing hockey, both in backyard rinks and in recreational leagues. Girls now have every bit as much chance to make great plays as the boys do, at all levels of hockey from rec league to pro.

It's today's kids who will write the next chapter of hockey's wonderful and hilarious history. What will your part be? Will it be *you* who becomes the Hayley Wickenheiser or Sidney Crosby of tomorrow?

INDEX

Abel, Sid, 68, 74
Abby Hoffman Cup, 93
Adams, Charles, 60
Allan Cup, 39, 56
Allan, Sir H. Montagu, 39
Amateur Hockey Association of
    Canada, 20, 25, 33
Amonte, Tony, 130
Anaheim Mighty Ducks, 123
Anderson, Glenn, 114
Armstrong, George, 91
Art Ross Trophy, 87
Asia, 5
Atlanta Flames, 103
bagataway, 11
ball and stick games, 4–10
Ballard, Harold, 107
banana blade, 17
bandy, 9–10
Benedict, Clint, 23
Bergman, Gary, 100
Birmingham Bulls, 106
Blainey, Justine, 120
Blake, Toe, 68
Boston Bruins, 60–61
    and Bobby Orr, 96–97
    and Phil Esposito, 102–103
    and Stanley Cup, 83, 97, 102
Botterill, Jennifer, 137
Boucher, Frank, 65
Boutette, Pat, 68
Brodeur, Martin, 128
Buffalo Sabres, 103
Burch, Billy, 62
Buzinski, Steve, 47
California Seals, 94
Campbell, Clarence, 77–79
Canadian Amateur Hockey
    Association, 48
Canadian Broadcasting Corporation
    (CBC), 70
Canadian Hockey Association, 40
Canadian Women's Hockey League
    (CWHL), 124
Cannon, Jimmy, 20
Challenge Cup, 32, 33, 39
Cherry, Don, 94, 103

Chicago Blackhawks, 66–67, 70
    and Bobby Hull, 85–86
CHUM Witch, 84
Cincinnati Stingers, 106
Clancy, King, 72–73
Clark, Wendel, 68
Clarke, Bobby, 99, 100
Coffey, Paul, 114
Cold War, 99
Coloured Hockey League, 25
Colville, Mac, 67
Colville, Neil, 67
Cook, Bill, 65
Cornwall Victorias, 52, 53
Cournoyer, Yvan, 101
Courtnall, Russ, 68
Creighton, James, 13
Crosby, Sidney, 137, 140, 142–143
Cusimano, Pete, 66
Czechoslovakia, 121
Dartmouth, NS, 25
Dartmouth Chebuctos, 25
Davidson, Gary, 104–105
Davidson, Melody, 136
Dawson City, YT, 34
Dawson City Nuggets, 34–36
Daytona Aeros, 106
Dee, James, 37
Detroit Cougars, 66
Detroit Red Wings, 66, 68, 74
    and Gordie Howe, 80
Dill, Bob, 76–77
Dionne, Marcel, 68
Doran, Pat, 40–41
draft system, 85
Dryden, Dave, 17
Dwyer, Bill, 62–64
East Division, 94
Eastern Canada Hockey Association
    (ECHA), 25, 37, 40
Edmonton Oilers, 106
    and Wayne Gretzky, 114–115
Egypt, 4
England, 9–10
equipment, 16–24
Esposito, Phil, 99, 101, 102–103
Evans, Trent, 129

fans, 44, 52, 95, 104
fighting, 27–28
Finland, 21
Flaman, Fernie, 77
Florida Panthers, 44, 123
forward lines, 67–68
Franklin, John, 14
Fredrickson, Frank, 49, 56, 57
Fuhr, Grant, 114
Garneau, Marc, 109
Geoffrion, Bernie, 85
Gibson, "Doc" John L., 36–37
Gilbert, Rod, 68
gloves, 19
Golden Age of Hockey, 73–74
Great Depression, 59, 67, 79
Greece, 5
Gretzky, Wayne, 53, 111–117, 128, 132
Habs. See Montreal Canadiens
Hadfield, Vic, 68
Haliburton, Thomas Chandler, 12
Halifax Rules, 25
Hamilton Tigers, 60, 62
Hartford Whalers, 106
Hat Trick, 43
helmets, 21
Henderson, Paul, 100
Henie, Sonja, 82
Henry, Camille "the Eel," 77
Henry, "Sugar Jim," 83
Hewitt, Foster, 69–70, 76
hockey bags, 16, 24
hockey cards, 53
Hockey Night in Canada, 69–70
hockey's name, 15
hockey sticks, 3, 4, 11, 16–18
hockey tape, 18
hockey terms, 42, 43
Hoffman, Abby, 92–93
Horton, Tim, 89
Howe, Gordie, 68, 79–80
Hull, Bobby, 17, 85–87
Hull, Brett, 128
hurley, 6–7
Iceland, 5
Iginla, Jarome, 130, 139, 140
Imlach, George "Punch," 17
indoor ice rinks, 26
indoor leagues, 25, 26
International Hockey League, 36–37
Ireland, 6–7

Iron Curtain, 120–122
Joliat, Auriele, 62
Joseph, Curtis, 128
Kaleta, Alex, 43
Kane, Patrick, 139, 140
Kansas City Scouts, 103
Kariya, Paul, 129, 130
Kelly, Red, 108
Kenora Thistles, 60
keretizein, 5
Kesler, Ryan, 139
Kharlamov, Valeri, 99, 100
King, Jason, 68
Kingston, ON, 13, 25
Kurri, Jari, 114
labour dispute, 134–135
Lach, Elmer, 68
Lalond, Ada, 52
Lalonde, "Newsy," 46, 53
Langenbrunner, Jamie, 140
Lapensée, Albertine, 52–53
Laviolette, Jack, 46
Leeman, Gary, 68
Lemieux, Mario, 31, 125–127, 128, 129
LeSueur, Percy, 38
Lindros, Eric, 68, 128
Lindsay, Ted, 68
Livingstone, Eddie, 54
Lizhniki Ice Palace, 99
Lord Stanbot, 33
Los Angeles Kings, 68, 94
    and Wayne Gretzky, 115–116
Lucky Loonie, 129, 132
Luongo, Roberto, 140
Madison Square Garden, 45, 63, 106
Mahovlich, Pete, 99, 101
Malone, "Phantom," Joe, 46
Maple Leaf Gardens, 50, 58, 59, 69–70,
    99, 107
masks, 22–23
Masterton, Bill, 21–22
McGee, "One–Eyed" Frank, 36, 49
McGill University Hockey Club, 25
McKenzie, Jim, 6
McLaughlin, Major Frederic, 67
Meeking, Gordon, 51
Mellanby, Scott, 44
Messier, Mark, 114
Mikhailov, Boris, 100
Mikita, Stan, 17
Minnesota North Stars, 94

Mogilny, Alexander, 122
Molson, 110
Montreal, QC, 13, 14, 25, 54
Montreal Amateur Athletic
    Association, 32–33
Montreal Canadiens, 39–41, 44–45, 54,
    60, 62, 68, 72, 77–79, 110
    and Stanley Cup, 31, 83, 87
    and Toronto Maple Leafs, 87–88,
        89–90
Montreal Forum, 78–79, 99
Montreal Hockey Club, 32–33
Montreal Maroons, 60, 61
Montreal Rules, 25
Montreal Wanderers, 38–41, 52, 54, 60
Montreal Westerns, 52
Morenz, Howie, 72
Morrison, George, 108
Murphy, Dennis, 104–105
National Hockey Association (NHA),
    37, 39, 41, 45, 48, 51, 54
National Hockey League (NHL), 44,
    54–55, 73–74
    American teams join, 60–67
    expansion of, 93–95, 103–106, 123
    international players join, 102,
        120–121
    labour dispute with, 134–135
National Hockey League Players'
    Association (NHLPA), 95–96, 134–135
National Women's Hockey League
    (NWHL), 124
Native games, 10–11
New York Americans, 62–63, 64–65
New York Islanders, 103
New York Raiders, 106
New York Rangers, 31, 63–65, 67, 68
    and Howie Morenz, 72
    and Phil Esposito, 103
    and Wayne Gretzky, 116
nicknames, 46–47, 67–68
Norris, James E., 66
Northern Fusiliers, 51
Northwest Passage, 14
Notre Dame Hounds, 68
Oatman, Eddie, 51
O'Brien, Ambrose, 39–41
octopus, legend of, 66
Olympic hockey, 56, 98
    1920 Olympics, 57
    1980 Olympics, 118–119

1998 Olympics, 124, 127–128
2002 Olympics, 127–134
2010 Olympics, 136–140
Ontario Hockey Association (OHA),
    25, 50, 51
Ontario Professional Hockey Leagues, 37
oochamkunutk, 11
Original Six, 74, 94
Orr, Bobby, 96–97
Ottawa Hockey Club, 34, 36
Ottawa Senators, 38, 54, 60, 123
Pacific Coast Hockey Association
    (PCHA), 48, 59
paganica, 5
Parise, Zack, 140
Patrick, Frank, 48
Patrick, Lester, 48, 65, 80
Peca, Mike, 128
Perry, Corey, 139
Philadelphia Flyers, 68, 94, 95
Pitre, Didier "Cannonball," 46
Pittsburgh Penguins, 94
    and Mario Lemieux,125–126
    and Sidney Crosby,143
Pittsburgh Pirates, 64
Plante, Jacques, 23
Pocklington, Peter, 115
Poile, Bud, 95
Poulin, Marie–Philip, 137
Preston Rivulettes, 71
professional hockey, 36–37, 38, 39
pucks, 3, 4, 19–20, 60, 74
Pulford, Bob, 90
Quakenbush, Bill, 83
Quebec Bulldogs, 54
Quebec Hockey Club, 25
Quebec Nordiques, 106
radio, 69–70
Rafalski, Brian, 128, 131, 140
Rankin Inlet, NU, 31
Ranscombe, Hilda, 71
Ranscombe, Nellie, 71
Ratelle, Jean, 68
referees, 67
Renberg, Mikael, 68
Renfrew Creamery Kings, 40, 41, 45
Rhéaume, Manon, 124
Richard, Maurice "Rocket," 68, 75–76,
    77, 83, 85
Richard Riot, 78–79
Rickard, Tex, 45, 63

Roenick, Jeremy, 131
Rome, 5, 6
Romnes, Edwyn "Doc," 70
Rutherford, Alexander, 18
Sakic, Joe, 128, 131
San Francisco Sharks, 106
San Jose Sharks, 123
Sawchuk, Terry, 90
Scotland, 8–9
Scott, Herb, 22
Sedin, Daniel, 68
Sedin, Henrik, 68
Seibert, Earl, 76
Shibicky, Alex, 67
shin pads, 18–19
shinty, 8–9
Shore, Eddie, 61, 72–73
shootouts, 111, 135
Simmer, Charlie, 68
skates, 11, 21
Smith, Billy, 108
Smythe, Conn, 50–51, 58–59, 65, 70,
    75, 89
South America, 5
Soviet Union. *See* USSR
sponsorship, 84
Stanley, Allan, 91
Stanley, Isobel, 28–29
Stanley, Lord, 28, 29
Stanley Cup, 29–33, 38, 55, 57, 59–60,
    65, 76–77, 87, 97, 102
    1952 semi-final, 83
    1967 final, 88, 90–91
Stastny, Peter, 121–122
St. Louis Blues, 94
    and Wayne Gretzky, 116
sudden death overtime, 110–111, 135
Summit Series, 1972, 98–102
superstitions, 66, 84, 103, 129, 132
Suter, Gary, 128
Sutherland, Bill, 95
Sutherland, James Thomas, 13
Sutter brothers, 110
Szabados, Shannon, 136, 137
Taft, Sammy, 43
Tampa Bay Lightning, 103, 123, 124
Taylor, "Cyclone," 18
Taylor, Dave, 68

Team Russia, 128
television, 70, 74, 93
Toews, Jonathan, 139
Tootoo, Jordan, 31
Toronto Arena Company, 55, 58
Toronto Blueshirts, 54, 55
Toronto Maple Leafs, 22, 50, 58–59,
    68, 74
    and Montreal Canadiens, 77–79,
        87–88, 90–91
    Stanley Cup wins, 87
Toronto Shamrocks, 54
Toronto St. Pats, 50, 58, 60
Team USA, 99, 118–119, 128, 136,
    138–140
Team USSR, 99, 118–119
University of Toronto Hockey Team,
    28, 50, 56
USSR, 102, 121–122
Valiquette, Jack, 68
Vancouver Canucks, 68, 103
Vancouver Pacific Coliseum, 99
Vezina, Georges, 53
Victoria Cougars, 57, 60, 66
Waghorne, Fred, 67
Washington Capitals, 103
West Division, 94
Western Canada Hockey League
    (WCHL), 59
Western Hockey League (WHL),
    59–60, 66
Whelpley, James, 21
Wickenheiser, Hayley, 133–134
Williams, Tiger, 68
Windsor, NS, 12, 15
Winnipeg Arena, 99
Winnipeg Falcons, 56, 57
Winnipeg Jets, 106
women's hockey, 29, 52–53, 71, 92–93,
    119–120, 124, 133–134, 136–137
World Hockey Association (WHA),
    104–106, 110, 114
World War I, 48–53
World War II, 92
Yzerman, Steve, 131
Zamboni, 81–82
Zamboni, Frank, 81–82